Studies in Jungian Thought

JAMES HILLMAN, General Editor

Satan in the Old Testament

Rivkah Schärf Kluger
Translated by Hildegard Nagel

Northwestern University Press
Evanston 1967

LIBRARY OF CONGRESS CATALOG CARD NUMBER: 67–15935
Composed in Janson and Melior types, printed, and bound by Kingsport Press, Inc., Kingsport, Tennessee

The original German-language edition of SATAN IN THE OLD TESTAMENT was published in 1948 by Rascher Verlag of Zürich under the title "Die Gestalt des Satans im Alten Testament," as Part III of the volume by C. G. Jung, *Symbolik des Geistes*.

Man sagt, Gott mangelt nichts,
Er darf nicht unsrer Gaben;
Ist's wahr, was will er dann
Mein armes Herze haben?

ANGELUS SILESIUS

CONTENTS

FOREWORD

As the psychology of the unconscious advances, it seems to move into ever deeper realms. Perhaps this is to be expected from "depth" psychology. But this descent also compels psychology to investigate the dark and demonic aspects of the psyche which lie below collective life and within our personal problems. As the investigation in depth proceeds through a psychotherapeutic analysis, that which begins as a personal problem sooner or later tends to reveal demonic or mythological characteristics. In the language of C. G. Jung, at the core of every personal complex is something mythical, something archetypally collective, which both constellates personal troubles to be enacted and re-enacted in set forms and gives to these problems their drama and their meaning.

For this reason, and for others too, "getting to the bottom" of a psychological issue requires research into the fundamentals of the psyche. Not only do we need to observe its demonic depths through case material and psychopathological behavior; we also need to know how the psyche operates in and for itself at levels beyond personal consciousness. Myths, folktales, and religious texts present just such operations of the psyche at its impersonal objective level. In this kind of psychological material the influences of personal consciousness have been purified out through the filters of time while the essentials have been retained through the crystallizing effect of tradition. Further, religious myths and tales continue to give meaning to psychological events. They continue to be reflected in the spontaneous dreams and visions of people today who may never have been directly influenced by religious dogma or practice. The deepening of psychology involves it inescapably with religion. The history of religion—even its archaeology and philology—takes on new significance in the light of its new role: that of amplifying the background for understanding the archetypal depths of the psyche. No longer is it a matter of psychologizing religion and reducing religious events to "only psychological" case studies. Rather, psychology cannot get to the bottom of its own field without help from research in religion.

The issue of evil, for instance, lies not only in the province of moral philosophy and theology. Evil is involved in practical psychology, in clinics and consulting rooms, since it is just because something has gone "wrong" or is no longer "good" that a person goes to psychotherapy in the first place. Within the personal complexes of what is "wrong" or "bad" and the ills and devils that beset us is concealed the age-old question of what is evil—and what is its relation to God, to the world, and to man. A study of the figure of the biblical Satan becomes necessary in our search for answers.

In this monograph, Rivkah Schärf Kluger investigates Satan from a psychological viewpoint which leads to far-reaching reflections on the nature of the God-image in the Old Testament. Her research achieves two major aims. First, it shows how the image of Satan goes through a development which can be seen as a development of consciousness within the Old Testament image of God. Second, this study illumines the significance of the inner enemy and accuser. Satan interferes, opposes, and accuses. As an instrument of conflict he is fundamental to consciousness, which arises from tension. Further, Satan, while representing that demonic archetypal process associated with the Godhead that sets destruction going, is revealed through this study to have a final purpose which is not just evil in the usual sense. An aspect of this finality may be the development—in both God and man—of self-limitation through self-opposition.

This monograph formed a separate section in one of Jung's books, *Symbolik des Geistes,* the other three parts of which are now in Volumes IX, XI, and XIII of his *Collected Works.* Jung did much work in collaboration with other scholars. The writings of these collaborators are not included in the *Collected Works of C. G. Jung*, yet, if his spirit is to be truly represented in the English language, the writings of his co-workers should also be available. It is with this aim also in mind that we are pleased to bring this study to the English-reading public as a volume in the series "Studies in Jungian Thought."

JAMES HILLMAN

PREFACE TO THE AMERICAN EDITION

THIS WORK originally appeared in German in 1948 as a part of C. G. Jung's volume *Symbolik des Geistes,* published by Rascher Verlag, Zürich.

Since then it has often been suggested that I publish it in English, because its subject is of immediate relevance to the religious and psychological problems of our age. But time and circumstances did not, until recently, allow me to focus on this endeavor. However, the intervening years have not appreciably changed the spiritual and psychological problem with which this work is concerned; it has, if anything, become intensified, and, although some slight glimmerings of progress are beginning to be discernible, the solution is still far off.

The lines of thought which have directed my understanding of the material I owe to the psychology of C. G. Jung, to whom I feel most deeply indebted. If I have succeeded in coming nearer to the meaning of this great material, it is due to his psychological and particularly his religious-psychological insights, which have given me the key to it.

An examination of the more recent literature has convinced me that my thesis has not become outdated. (See especially the article "Satan," by Th. H. Gaster, in *The Interpreter's Bible* [Nashville: Abingdon Press, 1963], and the bibliography cited there; and Koehler-Baumgartner, *Lexikon in veteris testamenti libros* [Leiden: E. J. Brill, 1958], *sub verbo.*) This encourages me to present my conclusions in the English language to interested readers.

In order not to burden this book with additional references, I have added only such views and material as are of primary importance to my subject.

I have used the King James translation for Bible quotations, except in certain instances, duly noted, where it is not as accurate as other versions. In all cases, however, the term "the Lord" has been replaced by the original Hebrew designation of the name of God, "Yahweh," and the term "angel of the Lord" by "*mal'āk Yahweh*," which seems preferable in a work dealing with theological categories.

Quotations from French and German have been translated. All Hebrew, Arabic, and Syrian words have been transcribed. Transcriptions contained in quotations have been left in the form chosen by their authors. Hebrew names from the Old Testament are given in the form used in the quoted translations of the Bible.

Los Angeles RIVKAH SCHÄRF KLUGER
February, 1967

ACKNOWLEDGMENTS

As this American edition goes to press I wish to express my gratitude to my dear friend Alice Crowley for her great interest, encouragement, and assistance, both moral and material, in the preparation of this translation. I also wish to thank Fowler McCormick for generously helping defray the costs involved in enabling this book to appear. I am grateful to Dr. James Hillman for his warm and active interest in this English-language edition and seeing it through to completion. To Hildegard Nagel go my special thanks for the personal devotion and great care with which she translated this book. I am indebted to Mrs. Janet Dallett for her secretarial assistance and especially for her painstaking preparation of the Index. Last and not least I want to express my thanks to my husband, whom I consulted throughout the preparation of this American edition, for his generous advice and assistance.

R. S. K.

LIST OF ABBREVIATIONS

BZAW	*Beihefte zur Zeitschrift für die alttestamentliche Wissenschaft.* 1896——.
HSAT[4]	*Die Heilige Schrift des Alten Testaments.* Trans. E. Kautzsch *et al.* Ed. A. Bertholet, in connection with the previous collaborators and Prof. Eissfeldt. 2 vols. Tübingen: Mohr, 1922.
KAT	Eberhard Schrader, *Die Keilinschriften und das Alte Testament.* Ed. H. Winckler and H. Zimmern. 3d ed. Berlin, 1903.
RGG[2]	*Die Religion in Geschichte und Gegenwart. Handwörterbuch für Theologie und Religionswissenschaft.* Ed. Hermann Gunkel and Leopold Zscharnak, in connection with A. Bertholet *et al.* 5 vols. Tübingen: Mohr, 1927–31. 2d ed., 1928.
ZAW	*Zeitschrift für die alttestamentliche Wissenschaft.* Berlin, 1881——.
ZDMG	*Zeitschrift der Deutschen Morgenländischen Gesellschaft.*

Introduction

1. *Problem and Method of Approach*

We live in a time which has seen evil darkening the world and manifesting a hitherto unsuspected power, evoking St. John's apocalyptic vision of Satan unchained after his thousand years' bondage (Rev. 20:2, 3, 7, 8) as an adequate image of immediately experienced reality. The nature and origin of this force has become a terribly actual problem in our time. So it may not be meaningless to trace the image of the devil back to its origins.

This presupposes, however, that such mythologems be understood as spontaneous expressions of psychic reality, as symbols which are able to give adequate expression to what is beyond the grasp of reason. The assembling of all the statements concerning such a mythological figure as Satan permits us to perceive its structure and thereby the psychological content of which it is the symbolic expression. Such an understanding of mythologems rests on the further premise that the human psyche is not to be viewed as something inherently different from the "superhuman" (and also not from the "subhuman"), but as an organ corresponding to these spheres, which contains these nonhuman, super- and subhuman forces within itself. My subject will not be God and devil, not their essence as such—that would be metaphysical speculation—but the psychological contents and the experiences of the superhuman in a religiously creative time, whose expression they are. Not metaphysical entities, but their image in man's soul—God and the devil as primal images, archetypes of the human psyche, will be the object of my observations. I base my conception on the fundamental views of C. G. Jung concerning this problem. In his Introduction to *The Tibetan Book of the Dead* [1] he says in this regard:

> Metaphysical assertions, however, are *statements of the psyche,* and are therefore psychological. To the Western mind, which compensates its well-known feelings of resentment by a slavish regard for "rational" explanations, this obvious truth seems all too obvious, or else it is seen as an inadmissible negation of metaphysical "truth." Whenever the Westerner hears the word "psychological," it always sounds to him as "only psychological." For him the "soul" is something pitifully small, unworthy, personal, subjective, and a lot more besides.

And in *Psychology and Alchemy* [2] he writes:

> However we may picture the relationship between God and soul, one thing is certain: that the soul cannot be "nothing but." On the contrary it has the dignity of an entity endowed with, and conscious of, a relationship to Deity. Even if it were only the relationship of a drop of water to the sea, that sea would not exist but for the multitude of drops. . . . As the eye to the sun, so the soul corresponds to God. . . . It would be blasphemy to assert that God can manifest himself everywhere save only in the human soul. Indeed the very intimacy of the relationship between God and the soul automatically precludes any devaluation of the latter.[3] It would be going perhaps too far to speak of an affinity; but at all events the soul must contain in itself the faculty of relation to God, i.e., a

1. C. G. Jung, *Psychology and Religion: East and West*, in *Collected Works* (Bollingen Series XX [New York, Pantheon Books]), XI (1958), 511 f.

2. C. G. Jung, *Psychology and Alchemy*, in *Collected Works* (Bollingen Series XX), XII (1953), 10–11.

3. "The fact that the devil too can take possession of the soul does not diminish its significance in the least" (*ibid.*, p. 11, n. 1).

> correspondence, otherwise a connection could never come about. This correspondence is, in psychological terms, the archetype of the God image.

This correspondence alone, as it found its expression in biblical texts, will be my subject of discussion. And insofar as these texts depict a development in the concept of God, one may, in this sense, speak also of God's fate in the human soul, without this being misinterpreted as a blasphemy. Moreover, this study, which is dedicated to a scholarly investigation, will leave untouched the ultimate metaphysical question as to whether there is a metaphysical reality corresponding to the inner-psychic process of a developing God image.

It might perhaps be said here, however, that through the breadth and depth of Jung's concept of the soul—it is for him of "limitless range and unfathomable depth" [4]—the ancient problem of transcendence and immanence has lost acuteness, since immanence, so understood, includes the effects, the imprint, or whatever we want to call it, of that which extends beyond the human; that is, of the transcendent. The transcendent is met from the background of one's own psyche. But whatever position is taken in regard to the transcendence problem, a scientific investigation must necessarily limit itself to the *phenomenon* of the God image as it emerges from the texts. From the transcendental standpoint too, God can only be apprehended in the existential form of a psychic content, in the refraction of human vision. Even if the opposition between the "immanent" and the "transcendent" conception of God is considered as essential and valid, it ceases to exist in the realm of science, i.e., in the attention directed to the *phenomenon* of the *image of God.* In this phenomenon, which is all that man can grasp, these two planes of conception, i.e., immanence and transcendence, overlap.

Such an understanding of the development of the God image in the human psyche presupposes an unprejudiced

4. *Ibid.*, p. 13.

consideration of all statements referring to this phenomenon with all its pertinent connections. Where suprapersonal contents have acquired the quality of personality, as is the case in the Old Testament, they can be understood only in terms of personality structure and its whole pattern of interrelations. The figure of Satan, which concerns us here, can therefore never be grasped "in itself," but only in its relation to God. Its nature can become clear only in relation to God in all his aspects. It is, for instance, altogether inadequate to rest content with having established that, in the story of Job, Satan is subordinate to God. That is one single aspect of the relation between Satan and God in the Old Testament. It remains a colorless statement as long as the nature and degree of this dependence, itself depending on the nature of God and of Satan, is not brought to light out of the total biblical text.

Hence the questions arise: How does Satan appear in the Old Testament? How did this concept come about? And what is its significance in Old Testament theology?

Methodologically, the later, post–Old Testament development of Satan, though it may motivate the investigation, cannot be its point of departure. It is true that if we approach our material with questions from "outside," from later or parallel connections, like the one mentioned before—whether or not Satan is subordinate to God—it will answer us. But the nature of Satan will not be disclosed by such a procedure. My aim is to put the questions arising from the material itself, to look at the statements about Satan as pieces of mosaic that must be carefully fitted together to form a picture. And every established character trait will be studied for its significance to the material as a whole.

2. *Survey of the Literature on the Problem*

SATAN APPEARS as a distinct mythological personality in only a few Old Testament passages (Job 1:6–12 and 2:1 ff.; Zech. 3:2 ff. and II Chron. 21:1) which, especially the passages in Job, have been discussed by numerous commentators. The present study will refer to them when dealing with the individual passages and critically evaluate their conclusions. However, the vastness of the theme and the extensive literature on each of the exegetic problems that will concern us preclude my mentioning all the available material.

In recent years only a few monographic studies have been devoted to this problem. Among the older ones, Gustav Roskoff's *Geschichte des Teufels* [5] especially must be mentioned. The chapter on the Old Testament Satan [6] may well be called a small monograph.[7] In spite of the orientation to his main theme of dualism in religions, Roskoff in many respects does justice to the specific character of the Old Testament Satan and contributes notably to the understanding of the principal aspect of the problem. For instance, at the very outset he affirms that the figure of Satan in the Book of Job "shows a significant turning point in the Hebrew concept"—an observation sufficient in itself to make it impossible "to believe this writing to be one of the oldest in Hebrew literature." [8] In the Satan of I Chronicles 21, Roskoff sees the "destructive quality of Jahwe already separated from himself . . . while in earlier passages it was still identified with him." [9] Correspondingly, in contrast to many a later author (see below, p. 45, nn. 85, 86), he is aware of the essential difference, on the one hand between Satan and Azazel (to whom he devotes the preceding chapter [10]) and, on the other, between the *šēdīm, śe 'īrīm,* and Lilith.[11] The latter are ghostly beings, such as play a role among other peoples, too; while the significance of Satan is to be sought in his relation to Yahweh. Roskoff believes that a

5. G. Roskoff, *Geschichte des Teufels,* 2 vols. (1869).
6. *Ibid.*, I, 186–99.
7. A more recent parallel to Roskoff's work is a book by Edward Langton, *Satan, a Portrait: A Study of the Character of Satan through All the Ages* (London, 1945). Langton provides, in condensed form, a good survey of the concepts of Satan during the course of the centuries. In the wide frame of his book the Old Testament is given so little space that this reference should be sufficient in our context.
8. Roskoff, *op. cit.*, p. 186. On this problem, see below, pp. 82 f.
9. *Ibid.*, p. 188.
10. *Ibid.*, pp. 177 ff.
11. *Ibid.*, p. 196.

Persian influence on the Satan figure is possible, but lays stress on the essential differences between it and the Persian Angra Mainyu. In his view the Persian influence is made ineffective by the supremacy of Yahwism.[12]

Although important contributions toward the understanding of the Old Testament Satan and his position within Yahwism are present in Roskoff's broadly conceived *Geschichte des Teufels*, other aspects of the Satan problem which are not immediately related to its main theme of dualism are naturally missing. In particular, the origin and the character of the Satan concept in the Old Testament itself and the detailed exegetic research which would have to go with it are not considered. Roskoff contents himself with the statement that there is no mention in the Old Testament of "how Satan became what he is,"[13] although a thorough study of the passages concerned offers much toward a solution of the problem. Roskoff's merit lies mainly in his dealing with questions of principle. He is directed toward an essential understanding of the Satan concept within Yahwism and attempts to perceive an inner-Yahwistic development of this figure (Azazel as the personification of impurity, Satan as inculpator in the Book of Job and as accuser and angel of retribution in Zechariah 3),[14] always with due, yet not one-sided, consideration of the religious-historical aspect. Even though I do not always agree with his every statement,[15] Roskoff seems to me to be a pioneer of a modern phenomenological approach which the present study will also endeavor to follow.

Hans Duhm—although his work, "Die bösen Geister im Alten Testament,"[16] deals with all the material related to the

12. *Ibid.*, p. 197. On the problem of Persian influence, see below, pp. 155 ff.

13. *Ibid.*, p. 189.

14. *Ibid.*, p. 197.

15. I cannot, for example, entirely agree with this line of development. In my opinion the development of the Satan figure does not begin with Azazel, but in the premythological use of the Satan concept. Its beginning can be understood only through the analysis of the concept throughout the Old Testament, an analysis lacking in Roskoff.

16. Diss., Tübingen, 1904.

problem and provides a good summary of it—does not work through to a grasp of the phenomenon "Satan" or even of evil in the Old Testament. Any real understanding is hampered at the outset by his purely external classification of the various figures. He groups the demonic figures according to their outer appearance, as theriomorphic, anthropomorphic, or of indistinct form. According to him, Satan belongs to the last group and therefore has no special significance. Such an external approach throws no light on the nature of the phenomena, so it is not surprising that Duhm's main conclusion—at least insofar as Satan is concerned—is incorrect. He writes: "One could think away the sum total of cacodemonic concepts in the Old Testament without receiving the impression that the character of even the old folk religion, let alone that of the prophets, would thereby be essentially altered." [17] This conclusion stops short at the outermost periphery of the problem. The fact that evil in the Old Testament is not primarily expressed in cacodemonic figures is precisely what brings up the essential problem of how it is expressed and what this form of expression means in regard to the essence of Old Testament religion. Duhm lays stress, as a positive factor, on the sober good sense of the Israelite people, which, in all essentials, was resistant to cacodemonic concepts. "The religion, not only of the prophets, but of all free men, was lived in the sober light of day, and had that conscious or unconscious moral tendency which granted only limited play to anything mystical." [18] And in another place: ". . . but the ancient peasant folk, as long as it was still intact, had little fear of malicious beings; in most cases it ascribed misfortune, too, to the anger of its God." [19] But Duhm here fails to see that this was only possible for this people because it experienced the demonic in its God, and not because it denied the demonic in the world and the soul.[20] Thereby he belittles the

17. Hans Duhm, *op. cit.*, p. 65.
18. *Ibid.*, pp. 65–66.
19. *Ibid.*, p. 65.
20. His underestimation of the significance of the cacodemons is justly contested by H. Kaupel (*Die Dämonen des Alten Testaments*

problem in favor of a morally evaluated "sober good sense."

Paul Volz, in his fine monograph *Das Dämonische in Jahwe*, has penetrated far more deeply into the problem.[21] He arrives at the essential conclusion, fully supported by biblical texts, that Yahweh was originally a demonic god, capable of assimilating, to some extent, many of the cacodemons which previously existed in popular belief. Accordingly, what is specific is not the absence of the demonic in the realm of Old Testament religious experience but the concept of an ambivalent god, the mingling of light and dark, of good and evil, in the one divine personality. Hence, monotheism in its essence is not unity against multiplicity as its absolute opposite; it is rather the *unity of multiplicity*. Multiplicity is at one and the same time overcome by and contained in unity. To be sure, the concept of a single divine personality is the outstanding achievement of the Old Testament, but this concept has had its own special fate, interwoven with the origin and further development of the Satan concept, as I shall try to show in what follows.

A Catholic counterpart of Hans Duhm's work may be seen in Heinrich Kaupel's *Die Dämonen des Alten Testaments*.[22] This author scores a point initially by putting the principal question of the meaning of Satan in the Old Testament framework itself, in conscious opposition to an exclusively religious-historical orientation. He refers to the "pattern of evolution" [23] still so obstinately rooted in the Old Testament field in which it has almost become a dogma; and he justifiably criticizes Hans Duhm's work as showing "very little real

---

[1930], p. 23; for further discussion of this book, see below). Even from the standpoint of religious and cultural history, it is doubtful whether the psychic disposition of the Jordan peasants was a different one. The prohibitions from Leviticus to Chronicles point to the contrary: "In all these passages, strong inclinations of the people are taken for granted; one does not go on and on rubbing in the same laws on account of insignificant things."

21. P. Volz, *Das Dämonische in Jahwe* (1924).
22. Kaupel, *op. cit.*
23. *Ibid.*, p. 7.

appreciation of the belief in Satan." [24] But in the end we are equally disappointed with this author, for, along with the all-too-leveling religious-historical standpoint, he also discards the assumption of any *development* in the Satan concept in question. By this opposite form of one-sidedness, Kaupel arrives at conclusions which have no more connection with questions arising from the material found in the Old Testament itself than do those of Duhm, though in his case the "external" approach is more from the side of dogma. Thus, his investigation leads to the thesis that the Satan of the Old Testament was, from the beginning, the same figure that is encountered in the New Testament, only not yet so clearly defined.[25] It is not surprising that he often takes questionable liberties with the material in order to prove this point. (For his thesis in detail see below.) However, in spite of the fact that Kaupel's investigation misses the point, as it seems to me it does, it contains certain valuable observations which shall be referred to in the relevant context. His comprehensive discussion of the literature on the subject is also of value.

In Anton Jirku's work, *Die Dämonen und ihre Abwehr im Alten Testament*,[26] we find the religious-historical and "absolute" standpoints side by side in unconcerned unrelatedness. "Yahweh," he says on page 22, "was at all times always the same," and " . . . at the beginning we see clearly and distinctly the miracle when as if from Heaven there came to a little desert people a God who would in time conquer half the

24. *Ibid.*

25. See *ibid.*, p. 99: "The author of the Book of Job has surely brought to expression this position of Satan (i.e., as adversary of man and God) which is drawn in even sharper outline in the New Testament." And on p. 117: "There is every ground for the assumption that the Tempter of the first of mankind and Satan are identical." "In Genesis 3 it says, not Satan, but serpent, only because the serpent was more generally familiar as a destructive and seducing being." Kaupel is probably not aware to what extent his interpretation rests upon the rationalistic assumption of an "author" manipulating this purely mythological story as seems to him best. Regarding the relation of the Paradise serpent and Satan, see below, pp. 49 f.

26. A. Jirku, *Die Dämonen und ihre Abwehr im Alten Testament* (1912).

world." Any demonic traits in Yahweh are categorically denied, as a rule, by quite naïvely begging the question. For instance, in regard to Numbers 12, where Moses' sister Miriam falls victim to leprosy, Jirku comments: "It is Yahweh who calls it down upon her. Naturally, what is meant is that he permits it." [27] According to Jirku, the attack on Moses (Exod. 4:24–26) is not to be ascribed to Yahweh either. "Although in its present form the story expressly names Yahweh as the one who attacks Moses and seeks to slay him, yet originally this would have referred, not to Yahweh, but to a night demon." [28] And further: "It cannot be assumed that the man who was the first to make Yahweh so wholly and completely the God of his people, who so to speak had daily intercourse with Yahweh, that this is the man of whom it is told that this very Yahweh sought to slay him." [29] The deep problem of divine ambivalence which appears in this story remains hidden from Jirku's all too narrow vision. That demonic actions are ascribed to Yahweh at all, Jirku says, is due to the existence of ancient demonic legends, "but . . . to the reviser the existence of other spirits beside Yahweh seemed impossible" and so "in pious zeal the demon was simply turned into Yahweh. . . ." [30] This process could not have been quite so "simple," however, even if it had really been a mere matter of a conscious literary procedure. If such expressly demonic traits could "simply" be ascribed to Yahweh, and that "in pious zeal," this again would be only another expression of the *inner* reality which Jirku would like to explain away, namely, that an identification of Yahweh with the ancient demons could be tolerated!

The greatest conceivable contrast to this "absolute" approach of Jirku's is shown by the rationalism of his explanation of the origin of belief in demons. "The terrors of the night led to the concept of night demons," [31] "the memories

27. *Ibid.*, p. 48.
28. *Ibid.*, p. 31.
29. *Ibid.*
30. *Ibid.*, p. 23.
31. Previously exemplified by Jirku in Gen. 32:23 ff. (*ibid.*, p. 28).

of the life spent in the wilderness to that of wilderness demons." [32] "The sudden incursions of disease gave rise to belief in disease demons, as the appearance of wild beasts to that in animal demons." [33] To Jirku, Satan figures as one of the disease demons because, in the Book of Job, "he appears as the creator of the various diseases which befall Job." [34] He concedes, however, that "Satan cannot be regarded as a mere demon of disease." But his conjecture that "he seems more to have been an evil spirit with special power over such demons" only goes to show that Jirku's point of departure cannot really come to grips with the problem of the Old Testament Satan.

Albert Brock-Utne, in his article "Der Feind," [35] pursues his investigations on quite different grounds from those of the aforementioned works. As is shown by the subtitle, "Die alttestamentliche Satansgestalt im Lichte der sozialen Verhältnisse des nahen Orients," he sees the roots of the Satan concept in the social sphere. He starts from those Old Testament texts where "Satan" indubitably refers to a man. Brock-Utne's undertaking is prejudiced by the fact that he does not approach these early passages impartially but sets out to prove that the metaphysical concept of Satan derived from Job and Zechariah and, restricted to the function of "accuser," was already present in the human sphere, with the end result that this definite human type of "accuser" was later transferred to the heavenly sphere. The social situation which gave rise to the type "Satan" is described by Brock-Utne as follows:

> Palestine—except for short intervals—was during all of antiquity a state fought over by great powers. The Pales-

32. *Ibid.*, p. 33, with reference to Azazel.
33. *Ibid.*, p. 96.
34. *Ibid.*, p. 49. The text speaks of only *one* sickness. The other blows come from Yahweh, not from Satan. In reference to this passage, see below, p. 125.
35. A. Brock-Utne, "Der Feind," *Klio, Beiträge zur Alten Geschichte,* XXVIII (1935). I am indebted to Professor W. Baumgartner of Basel for pointing out this work to me, as well as other literature "buried" in periodicals which relate to my theme.

> tinian princes were dependent upon this or that great king, or were under his influence; and the peace and prosperity of these princes and their realms were in many ways dependent upon the favor they could acquire with the great kings of Egypt or the countries along the Euphrates. Such a small Palestinian prince could therefore meet with great misfortune if some opponent *defamed* or *accused* him before the great king.[36]

Brock-Utne gives examples from the El-Amarna letters to support this view.[37] Hence these small princes lived in constant fear of the "slanderer." It was by slander before the great king that one princeling would try to eliminate another whose power he coveted. Brock-Utne gives a really imaginative description, substantiated by no text, of what such a slanderer was like:

> The slanderers were for the most part ambitious and ready-tongued nobles, whose abilities facilitated their admission to the court. They were mainly strong and courageous characters. One must picture them as aggressive and bold adventuring knights who acted with the wiliness that the situation demanded and the self-confidence befitting their noble origin.[38]

This mere conjecture becomes so much a certainty to Brock-Utne that he goes on to state: "Such men in particular were called 'satans.' " Such a "satan" was Hadad, who fled to Egypt and attained great favor with Pharaoh (I Kings 11:14 ff.); and a second was Rezon, who later became King of Damascus (I Kings 11:23 ff.). Jeroboam is accounted a third, in spite of his never being directly referred to as "satan." The first example raises doubts, since the Hadad story says nothing at all about any slanderous activity at Pharaoh's court but speaks only of this Edomite king's open *enmity* toward Solomon, which does not allow any other conclusion than to understand "satan" in this sense, i.e., as a *military foe.* The

36. *Ibid.*, p. 221.
37. *Ibid.*, pp. 221–22.
38. *Ibid.*, p. 222.

further example of Rezon makes Brock-Utne's interpretation altogether improbable. Aside from the fact that, from the context in this passage, the word *śāṭān* cannot mean anything other than "military adversary,"[39] there is another circumstance to consider. *Before* these "satans" rise up against Solomon, he has already written to Hiram, King of Tyre (I Kings 5:4): "But now Yahweh my God hath given me rest on every side, so that there is no adversary [literally "*śāṭān*"] nor evil occurrent." Here, too, it is clear that it is a question of military threat. Furthermore, Solomon would hardly recommend himself to another king of whom he wants something by asserting that no "satan," in Brock-Utne's sense, was against him. This would be a totally unsuitable argument, if only because he could not possibly know about it. It is in the nature of slander that the slandered learn of it only later, if ever; how can anyone know at a particular moment whether or not someone is intriguing against him?

Equally unconvincing is Brock-Utne's interpretation of *śāṭān* in I Sam. 29:4. According to him the Philistines are afraid that David will ingratiate himself with Saul at their expense. But it is clear from previous history that their distrust of David arises from the fact that he was formerly Saul's vassal. He might become their "adversary"; that is, he might desert to their adversary, Saul. Similar objections can be raised against Brock-Utne's interpretations of other passages.[40] Apart from these, a very important "satan" passage, namely Num. 22:22, cannot possibly be pressed into the accuser pattern. Brock-Utne refers to it, but without taking note of the doubt it throws on his theory.[41] Taking those passages in the

39. "And God stirred him up another adversary, Rezon the son of Eliadah, which fled from his lord Hadadezer king of Zobah: And he gathered men unto him, and became captain over a band . . . and they went to Damascus, and dwelt therein, and reigned in Damascus. And he was an adversary (*śāṭān*) to Israel all the days of Solomon . . ." (I Kings, 11:23 ff.).

40. *śitnā*, Ezra 4:6, as a very late passage, cannot serve as a proof of Brock-Utne's thesis. On II Sam. 19:22, see below, pp. 35 ff.

41. Brock-Utne, *op. cit.*, p. 227, n. 1.

Psalms (27:12; 71:13; 109:4, 20, 29) where the Satan concept occurs to be King-Psalms,[42] he uses them as a bridge to reach the conclusion "that the Satan figure has its roots in the political situation and in the cult of the kings." He sees the celestial Satan as simply a reflection of the political Satan:

> Yet in the course of time Yahweh himself became a great king. He was pictured as sitting in Heaven, surrounded by the court of the Sons of God; and it was natural that this court also acquired its figure of Satan. And, in conformity with the situation on earth, this Satan at the court of Yahweh was thought of as similar to the satans at earthly courts, namely, as a powerful noble—in this case a "Son of God"—who with self-assurance and eloquence traduces mankind.[43]

Brock-Utne here completely fails to recognize the *mythological* background of "the Sons of God." Another reason to doubt his conclusions is presented by the analogy, inescapable to every unprejudiced mind but ignored by him, between the situations in the Job Prologue and in I Kings 22:19 ff. The latter shows a prefiguration of the Job Satan which has nothing whatever to do with accusation.

Furthermore, Brock-Utne is overrationalistic in ascribing Satan's later importance to the fact that he was well suited to serve as a compromise between the trend inspired by the prophets, which saw all good and evil coming from Yahweh, and the belief of the broad primitive masses that evil was brought about by independent demons. It suited the monotheists to have Satan completely dependent on Yahweh; the rest of the people were satisfied by the nature of his functioning ("He went about and brought evil upon land and people" [44]).

Brock-Utne's book is of principal importance, it seems to me, in that it attempts to trace the concept and image of Satan through the *earlier* texts, that is, in the human sphere. But the attempt fails, in my opinion, because it projects a criterion

42. Brock-Utne bases his argument here largely on Birkeland, *Die Feinde des Individuums in der israelitischen Psalmenliteratur* (1933).
43. Brock-Utne, *op. cit.*, pp. 225 f.
44. *Ibid.*, p. 227.

derived from later texts—that of the "accuser" significance of Satan—into the earlier ones. Brock-Utne also deals in an all too simple manner with the problem of the Satan concept changing from the political into the celestial sphere. When he states that "the transition from human being to demon may have been helped along by the small chieftains, who, in their rage and fear, endowed their accusers with demonic traits," [45] he is merely going around in a circle. However, in principle his approach to the problem from the human sphere touches upon one of the most essential points in the problem of the Old Testament Satan. For this reason his attempt has some importance in spite of the inconclusiveness of his results.

Gerhard von Rad's point of departure is closely related to that of Brock-Utne.[46] He, too, derives the Satan concept from the social sphere, on the basis of an analysis of the word resulting in the meaning "foe, adversary." But, unlike Brock-Utne, he finds its origin in judiciary procedures rather than in political situations. According to his interpretation, Satan is in a very specific sense the accuser before the court of justice. Like Brock-Utne, who applies the slanderer concept to the earlier Satan passages, von Rad applies to them the *accuser* concept in its judicial form. The foes of Israel have a specific function before Yahweh: They are accusers of Israel. To von Rad this idea justifies the understanding of the satans whom Yahweh arouses against Solomon, not merely in the sense of "adversaries" but, here too, as possessing a definite juridical meaning: In the opinion of the Deuteronomic historian, Solomon had sinned, and it is in connection with this guilt that the satans arise during his reign.[47] Von Rad bases the concept of the adversary as "accuser" (*mazkīr ʿāwōn*) on Ezek. 21:23 ff. (Hebrew text, 21:28), which refers to Nebuchadrezzar as *mazkīr ʿāwōn*, and Ezek. 29:16, where the Egyptians are called *mazkīr ʿāwōn* (i.e., the person who brings their iniquity to

45. *Ibid.*, n. 2.
46. G. von Rad, art. "διάβολος," in Kittel, *Theologisches Wörterbuch zum Neuen Testament* (1933), II, 71–74.
47. *Ibid.*, p. 72.

remembrance with God). Aside from the fact that in these passages it says *śāṭān,* and not *mazkīr ʿāwōn,* and that there is no other foothold in this simple historic account for the theological problematics which von Rad has in mind, the same principal objections as were raised against Brock-Utne are valid here. Von Rad, too, takes from the Job Prologue what he assumes to be the decisive, specific meaning of the Satan concept, and then makes it appear as a mere analogy to situations on earth. "Like the earthly order, the heavenly order has likewise an organ in the High Court of God which assumes the office of a judicial accuser." [48] To von Rad the Satan in the Book of Job is "by no means a demonic being; he is the heavenly state official. . . ." [49] But he finds himself immediately obliged to limit this statement. "However, the concept of Satan in Job already implicitly contains the elements which later bent the line so deeply downward." [50] Going further still, in reference to the blows of fate dealt to Job by Satan, von Rad asserts: "Hence he is not *de facto* merely accuser, but has competences which reach beyond his juridical function. And here is an essential point where the analogy to the earthly *māzkīr ʿāwōn* fails." [51]

In order to reconcile Num. 22:22 with his theory, von Rad sees himself compelled to assume that perhaps the term *śāṭān* was not always applied to the same figure, so that in principle any one of the *benē hā-'elōhīm* could be appointed accuser. In Num. 22:22 it is even the Angel of Yahweh who comes to Balaam as Satan. Von Rad overlooks the fact that the accuser theory does not apply at all to the situation in the Balaam story. He does not, like Brock-Utne, simply evade the difficulties involved, but, as he considers the difficulties, he moves on increasingly shaky ground. He perceives, for instance, the

48. *Ibid.*
49. *Ibid.*
50. *Ibid.* To me it seems that the demonic elements in the Book of Job are very much in the foreground. See below, pp. 118 ff.
51. *Ibid.*

close inner connection of the *rūaḥ* concept in I Kings 22:19 ff. to the Job Prologue, and states:

> The difficulty consists in the fact that the very clear basic element of the accuser has next to nothing to do with the persecutor . . . and it is possible that in Israel there was the concept of an adversary who in certain situations was not only *de jure* associated with human sin but embodied the threat to their total existence.[52]

I Chron. 21:1 should have led von Rad to give up his thesis altogether, had he not allowed the problem to dissolve into a literary question. "I Chronicles 21, however, cannot be interpreted without further ado, since the context did not originally refer to Satan, but this concept came into the text only secondarily as a correction due to religious scruples." [53] In my opinion, it is just this change which opens up an unusually interesting problem (see below, pp. 160 f.). Yet von Rad himself sees in this passage a "difficult paradox which adheres to all belief in devils," and acknowledges that "this correction would hardly have been carried out in this way if the concept of Satan had not undergone a rather decisive transformation." [54]

Thus von Rad's basic thesis of Satan as juridical accuser is shown by the process of his own research to be insufficient. It would seem that he was ready for a far deeper comprehension of the Old Testament Satan than can be concluded from his article, when we find him making such profound formulations as the following: "Satan incorporates the threat to men from God, whether as accuser of their moral and religious failures or as a demonically destructive principle firmly anchored in the plan of salvation." [55]

Much the same approach as that of the two last-mentioned writers is shown by H. Torczyner in his article "How Satan

52. *Ibid.*, p. 73.
53. *Ibid.*
54. *Ibid.*
55. *Ibid.*, pp. 73–74.

Came into the World," [56] and by Adolphe Lods in his study "Les origines de la figure de Satan, ses fonctions à la cour céleste." [57] Though the mythological realm is their point of departure, they give primary attention to the problem of the earthly prototype and see the origin of the Satan figure in the historical situation. However, since they concern themselves mainly with the Job Prologue and Zech. 3:1 ff.—Torczyner seeing the origin of the Satan concept in Job and Lods leaning toward Zechariah—they do not really belong to this summary. We will return to them at the appropriate place (see below, pp. 30 ff.; pp. 135 f., etc.). Here I will mention only briefly the conclusions they reach. Torczyner sees in the Satan of the Book of Job a secret emissary of the Heavenly Court, corresponding to the secret emissaries of earthly kings, who come and go and report on the behavior of subjects.[58] He bases his view primarily on the derivation of the name Satan from the verb *šûṭ*, "to wander about"—an assumption which will be gone into exhaustively later (see below, pp. 30 f.). Lods summarizes the result of his research as follows: "1. Satan, in the vision of Zechariah, did not play the role of general advocate—since the judicial organization of the ancient Middle East did not seem to have had an official of that sort—but rather of the occasional accuser." (Opposed to this, see pp. 135 f.) "2. In the Job Prologue, the function of the *śāṭān* is that of an agent of the divine police." [59] He advances the latter concept in direct reference to Torczyner's aforementioned article, but without taking over that writer's etymological argument. He relies for the most part on historical parallels, which will be discussed later (see below, pp. 135 f.).

56. H. Torczyner, "How Satan Came into the World," *Expository Times* (1936–37), pp. 563 ff. This article also appeared as "Wie Satan in die Welt kam," *Mitteilungsblätter der Hebräischen Universität Jerusalem* (January, 1938), pp. 15 ff.

57. A. Lods, "Les Origines de la figure de Satan, ses fonctions à la cour céleste," *Mélanges Syriens offerts à M. R. Dussaud* (1939), pp. 649–60.

58. Torczyner, *op. cit.*, p. 16.

59. Lods, *op. cit.*, p. 660.

If we consider these works as a whole, they may perhaps be said to represent one-sided presentations of intrinsically important points of view. So perhaps it may be justifiable to attempt to assemble in one study the different points of view necessary for grasping the total phenomenon, in order to achieve a new phenomenological view of the whole, while naturally using as a basis the results of these previous investigations.

The Concept of "Satan" and Its Development in the Old Testament

1. *Etymology of the Word "Satan"*

IN THE WORLD of the Old Testament, names are not "sound and fume," but they have magic power; they are, so to speak, substantial and therefore, in effect, identical with the nature of their bearers. For example, in the creation story (Genesis 1 and 2), the giving of names to things is at the same time a bestowal of existence and essence. The power of names is also shown in the refusal to reveal one's name (Exod. 3:14; Gen. 32:29), because he who knows the name has power over him who bears it. This all suggests that with the figure of Satan, too, we inquire first into the meaning of his name.

It is generally accepted [1] that the name "Satan" comes from the verb *śāṭan*, "to persecute, be hostile to" and also, more specifically, "to accuse." In opposition to this there is found the opinion (in the *Historische Grammatik der hebräischen Sprache*, by H. Bauer and P. Leander [2]) that the noun belongs to the descriptive words with the suffix *-an* (> *on*). Gerhard von Rad [3] sets beside this deduction, which he refers to, the other possibility of a simple nominal formation *qāṭāl*, but he emphasizes that even in the latter case the verb *śāṭan* is proba-

1. See esp. Gesenius-Buhl, *Hebräisches und aramäisches Handwörterbuch über das Alte Testament* (1915) and Koehler-Baumgartner, *Lexikon in veteris testamenti libros* (Leiden: E. J. Brill, 1958).

2. 1922, p. 500 t.

3. Art. "διάβολος," in Kittel, *Theologisches Wörterbuch zum Neuen Testament* (1933), II, 71.

bly denominative. It is true that the verb appears only five times in the Old Testament, and those exclusively in the Psalms, in reference to "adversaries";[4] that is, it appears in later passages than the noun, which seems to support the assumption that the noun is the original and that the verb is derived from it. On the other hand, this theory is controverted by the circumstance that the secondary form of the verb *śāṭan*, *śāṭam*, is also found in five Old Testament passages: once in the Psalms,[5] once in the Book of Job,[6] and three times in Genesis,[7] in both Yahwistic and Elohistic passages.[8] The premise of the denominative is therefore not tenable, and with it von Rad's conclusion that the word "accordingly expresses a quality, not a function," loses its foundation. The noun *śiṭnā* also seems to me to offer evidence for the functional character of the word, since it can scarcely be interpreted otherwise than as an abstract noun of the function. The reference Gen. 26:21, where the word appears as the name of a well, probably of ancient origin, apparently derived from the verb *śāṭan*, again controverts the denominative theory of Bauer and Leander and von Rad. Moreover, aside from the question of

4. Ps. 38:20: "They also that render evil for good are mine adversaries [*yiśṭenūnī*, literally, "the ones who turn against me"]." Ps. 71:13: "Let them be confounded and consumed that are adversaries to my soul [*śōṭnē nafšī*]. . . ." Ps. 109:4: "For my love they are my adversaries [*yiśṭenūnī*]. . . ." Ps. 109:20: "Let this be the reward of mine adversaries [*pe'ullat śōṭnai*]. . . ." Ps. 109:29: "Let mine adversaries [*śōṭnai*] be clothed with shame. . . ."

5. Ps. 55:3: ". . . for they cast iniquity upon me, and in wrath they hate me [*ūbe-'af yiśṭemūnī*]. . . ."

6. Job 16:9: "He teareth me in his wrath, who hateth me [*'appō ṭāraf wai-yiśṭemēnī*]. . . ."

7. Gen. 27:41: "And Esau hated Jacob [*wai-yiśṭōm 'esāw 'et ya'aqōb*] because of the blessing wherewith his father blessed him." Gen. 49:23: "The archers have sorely grieved him, and shot at him, and hated him [*wai-yiśṭemūhū ba'alē ḥiṣṣīm*]. . . ." Gen. 50:15: "And when Joseph's brethren saw that their father was dead, they said, Joseph will peradventure hate us [*lū yiśṭemēnū yōsēf*] and will certainly requite us all the evil which we did unto him."

8. In reference to these passages, see *Die Heilige Schrift des Alten Testaments*, trans. E. Kautzsch (4th ed., A. Bertholet, 1922), referred to hereafter as *HSAT* [4].

grammar, the functional concept can be supported by individual study of the passages in question (cf. below, p. 57, concerning Num. 22:22).

Śāṭam, as the apparently older, secondary form, also offers a better starting point for investigating the word's fundamental meaning. The sense of "to persecute, to pursue," which emerges especially in Gen. 27:41 and 49:23, originally meant most concretely "to entrap," in the sense of setting a snare or a trap, or putting fetters on the feet.[9] The only Old Testament evidence for this basic meaning is in Hos. 9:8. There it says (of the prophet): *paḥ yāqōš 'al kol derākāw maśṭēmā be-bēt 'elōhāw* ("a snare of a fowler in all his ways, and hatred [*maśṭēmā*] in the house of his God").

Thus *maśṭēmā* appears in strict parallelism to *paḥ,* the birdcatcher's net. For this reason Guthe[10] translates it with "snares,"[11] in agreement with Gesenius.[12] However, a difficulty arises from the fact that *maśṭēmā* appears also in verse 7, and is made parallel to *'āwōn,* which would indicate a figurative meaning for *maśṭēmā,* too. Guthe translates it with *Sünde* ("sin)," as does the Zürich Bible. The latter, with its translation of *'āwōn* by *Anfeindung,* i.e., "persecution" ("hatred" in the King James version), adapts verse 8 to verse 7. But a figurative meaning in verse 8 disturbs the clear parallelism of the images. Wellhausen therefore deletes verse 8.[13] Gesen-

9. Gesenius, *Thesaurus Linguae Hebraeae et Chaldaeae Veteris Testamenti* (1840), col. 1327: "satam = insidiatus est alicui, hostiliter persecutus est eum. . . . Origo est in laqueo, vel potius decipulo ferreo ponendo, quo pedes prehendantur. . . ."

10. HSAT[4], II, 15.

11. Similarly, Karl Marti, *Das Dodekapropheton* (1904), p. 73.

12. *Thesaurus,* col. 1327: "maśṭēmā = compes, decipulum ferreum pedes alicuis prehendens."

13. *Die kleinen Propheten* (1898), p. 123. A real basis for this deletion is lacking, however. Wellhausen expressly rejects the derivation of *maśṭēmā* from "snare," as given in Gesenius, *Thesaurus,* again without giving his reason, insists upon "hatred" as the translation of *maśṭēmā,* according to verse 7, and declares it to be invalid for verse 8. He closes the gap with verse 9a: "*he'mīqū šiḥētū* belongs to verse 8, for, following *paḥ yāqōš* it cannot possibly be translated otherwise than by 'they have dug him a deep pit.' "

ius-Buhl [14] leaves the question of its authenticity open, but notes that to assert it would necessitate the deletion of verse 7. Marti [15] assumes that *maśṭēmā* is not the original word in the passage, with very good grounds, since *maśṭēmā*, even when taken as *Anfeindung*, is not a good parallel to *'āwōn* and may easily have slipped in from verse 8 in the place of some similar word. He believes this to have been *ḥaṭṭā'tām.*[16] Starting from the same principles, Guthe [17] arrives at a similar conjecture, and Ernst Sellin likewise grants verse 8 primary authenticity.[18] In my own opinion, the authenticity of verse 8 is supported in any case by the completeness of the parallel character of the images, for which *maśṭēmā* is structurally indispensable, while in verse 7 it is only loosely appended and does not seem absolutely necessary in the context of the meaning.

In this connection it is very interesting that, parallel to the noun *śāṭān*, *maśṭēmā* also became a name of the devil in late Judaism, as, for instance, in the Book of Jubilees (11:3 ff.; 17:16; 19:28; 22:16 ff.). He is the monarchical head of the evil spirits and plays essentially the role of the Old Testament Satan in his later development.[19]

The assumption of the authenticity of verse 8 gains support from the Syrian *śeṭam Pa.* = *compedivit, vinxit,*[20] which Sellin also points out (see above, n. 18), and *śūṭmā* = *compes,*

14. *Op. cit., s.v.*

15. Marti, *op. cit.*, p. 73.

16. *Ibid. ḥaṭṭā'ā* is in fact a usual parallel to *'āwōn;* see the following verse, 9b: "therefore he will remember their iniquity [*'awōnām*], he will visit their sins [*ḥaṭṭ'ōtām*]."

17. *HSAT* [4], II, 14, note to verse 7: "for *maśṭēmā* (= hatred) probably crept in from verse 8, read *ḥaṭṭā'tekā.*"

18. E. Sellin, *Das Zwölfprophetenbuch* (1921), p. 73: "*maśṭēmā* is found only here [i.e., verse 7] and in verse 8, but just after the latter passage the meaning of setting snares or persecution can be accounted as assured, chiefly according to the Syrian, probably in the concrete sense of fetters or sling."

19. See Bousset-Gressmann, *Die Religion des Judentums im späthellenistischen Zeitalter* (1926), p. 333.

20. See Gesenius, *Thesaurus, s.v.;* cf. also *Thesaurus Syriacus.*

vinculum pedum.[21] Now Arabic has the same meaning for *šaṭana,* which corresponds to the Hebrew *śāṭan.* It means, among other things, "to resist someone, to deter him from some intention, to bind him with the cord" (*šatn*).[22]

Consequently, by means of the basic meaning of the secondary form *śāṭam* and the Arabic *šaṭana* as parallel form to *śāṭan,* it can be concluded that the primal meaning of the verb *śāṭan* is *persecution by hindering free forward movement;* i.e., it means "to hinder, to oppose, an existing intention." This original meaning can probably be seen most clearly in Num. 22:22, where the *mal'āk Yahweh* literally crosses Balaam's intentions by standing in his way, *le-śāṭān lō.* The translation of the noun *śāṭān* by *Widersacher* ("adversary") in most passages by both the Zürich Bible and Luther therefore comes closest to the original meaning. Harry Torczyner, in his translation of the Bible,[23] renders the word as *Widergeist* ("adverse spirit"), which, it seems to me, is a concept derived from the much later mythological figure and not from the original, profane meaning of the word.

A number of earlier writers [24] advocated the thesis, already refuted by Gesenius and others,[25] that *śāṭān* is to be derived from *šūṭ,* "to rove about." [26] That this thesis had, in the last

21. See Gesenius, *Thesaurus;* also *Thesaurus Syriacus;* Brockelmann, *Lexicon Syriacum;* and Gesenius-Buhl, *op. cit., s.v. maśṭēmā:* "But if verse 8 is genuine, a derivation from the Syrian *śeṭam Pa.,* to bind with ropes . . . immediately suggests itself."

22. Adolf Wahrmund, *Handwörterbuch der arabischen und deutschen Sprache* (Giessen, 1877). Compare also the dictionaries of Lane, Belot, Kazimirski. The conjecture by Barth (*Etymologische Studien* [1893]) that *śāṭan* derives from *šatama* = "to slander," has already been rejected by Gesenius, *Thesaurus.*

23. H. Torczyner, *Die Heilige Schrift, neu ins Deutsche übertragen* (1937).

24. Herder, *Geist der hebräischen Poesie,* II, 19; Ilgen, *De libro Jobi,* pp. 125 ff.; *Simonis lex.,* ed. Eichhorn (see Gesenius, *Thesaurus*).

25. D. von Coelln, *Bibl. Theologie* (1896), I, 421, n. 35; Hengstenberg, *Christologie des Alten Testaments,* I, 34 (see Gesenius, *Thesaurus*).

26. So, for example, Ilgen, *op. cit.,* p. 128, n.: "Ex illo circumeundi, cursum per aliquod spatium conficiendi significatu, ortum est novum nomen *śāṭān,* ex hoc verbum *śāṭan.*"

analysis, to do with the theological interests of these older writers is shown clearly in Hengstenberg's refutation. According to him, they tried to show

> that the Satan of the Book of Job was not the Satan of the later books, but rather a good, pure angel, who merely had the office of an accuser, fiscal solicitor, or informant; basing their view upon the author's counting him, too, among the children of God; and that it was unfair to project the hatefulness of the office upon the person.[27]

Hengstenberg rejects this derivation upon grammatical grounds but in principle demonstrates the same theological interest in not tolerating Satan as such, i.e., as "adversary," among the angels. He merely makes it easier for himself by declaring that Satan could never have appeared among the angels; that was only a "poetic fiction," intended no more seriously by the author of the Book of Job than the idea that Yahweh should need to have a human being tested by Satan! The derivation of the noun *śāṭān* from *šūṭ* has also been stated by the Jewish scholar Samuel David Luzzatto: [28] "*teḥīlat qeriā'tō śāṭān miš-šūṭ bā-'āreṣ.*" More recently this has again been taken up by Harry Torczyner.[29] His argument, however, is not convincing. Along with other evidence, Torczyner cites the Arabic form *šaiṭān,* in which, according to him, the diphthong of the first syllable still shows its connection with a verb *šūṭ*, and not with *śṭn.* However, since the Arabic word is probably a borrowed biblical term, as will be shown (see pp. 32 ff.), it does not come into question as far as the origin of the concept is concerned. Torczyner continues:

> On the other hand, it is conceivable that the accusing activity of Shaitan [Torczyner takes *š* as the original form and refers to the change between *š* and *ś* in Hebrew

27. Hengstenberg, *op. cit.*, I, 35–36.

28. *Erläuterungen über einen Teil der Propheten und Hagiographen* (Lemberg, 1876), p. 197. I am indebted for this reference to Rabbi S. Speier, Zurich.

29. "How Satan Came into the World," *Expository Times,* XLVIII (1936–37), 564.

> and also between Hebrew and Arabic] or Satan led to the formation of a new verb, *stn,* which means "accuse, be hostile," and from which later a substantive, *sitna,* "accusation," developed.[30]

This statement, however, falls to pieces in the face of the fact that the derivation of the noun *śāṭān* from *šūṭ* and the concept of Satan as the roving messenger is taken from the relatively late Book of Job and the so-called folktale cannot, according to most scholars, be dated earlier than 600 B.C. (cf. pp. 95 ff.). But the noun *śāṭān* appears in much older texts (Num. 22:22; I Sam. 29:4; I Kings 5:18; 11:14, 23). This does not contradict the possibility of there being a conscious pun with the words *šūṭ* and *śāṭān,* perhaps even based on one of those false folk etymologies which are not uncommon in the Old Testament.

As was mentioned before, A. Lods, who accepts Torczyner's conception of the Job Satan as a roving divine "secret police agent," also draws the line at the latter's etymological disquisitions (". . . without accepting the adventurous etymological hypothesis of Mr. Torczyner . . .") [31] In his arguments, which I had not seen prior to my own analysis of Torczyner's hypothesis, I found my standpoint confirmed and supported by further evidence:

> Is it likely that the verb *sāṭan,* "to be opposed," and the substantive *siṭnā,* "opposition," which are verified to be from very early times, for example by the name of a well in the desert (Gen. 26:20), would be derived from a noun designating a police agent and consequently implying the existence of a centralized and organized State? The concurrence of the name of *sāṭān* and the verb *šouṭ,* "to circulate," in Job 1:7 may be, if it is intentional, a simple play on words by assonance, of which the Hebrew authors and writers were fond.[32]

30. *Ibid.*
31. A. Lods, "Les Origines de la figure de Satan, ses fonctions à la cour céleste," *Mélanges Syriens offerts à M. R. Dussaud* (1939), pp. 649–60.
32. *Ibid.*, pp. 658–59.

Beyond that, however, it can be demonstrated that the noun *śāṭān* belonged originally to the profane sphere. It is used with its profane meaning in texts older than those which depict the mythological Satan. This fact, which will be shown in what follows to be of far-reaching theological significance, is seemingly contradicted by another fact, namely, that the Arabic word *šaiṭān* does not turn up for the first time in the Koran, as a designation of the devil along with *Iblis*, but is also found in pre-Islamic writings as a synonym for the term *ǵinn*. This is also true for the plural form. Ignaz Goldziher gives evidence of *ǵinn* and *šaiṭān* being used with the specific meaning of the poet's daimonion.[33] Franz Praetorius believes it probable, on these grounds, that the Judeo-Christian Satan is of Arabic origin.[34] In this he opposes Wellhausen, who regards *šāiṭān* as a Christian term which penetrated Arabic from Abyssinia,[35] and D. H. Müller, who holds the Arabic *šaiṭān* to be one of the oldest derivatives of the Hebrew *śāṭān*.[36] A. S. Tritton mentions that the Arabic philologists held *šaiṭān* to be an Arabic word.[37] They derived it from the root *sh-ṭ-n;* a few, however, leaned toward the root *sh-y-ṭ*.[38] Tritton, however, believes it probable, since the concept is clearly borrowed, that the word—a regular Arabic form—is also borrowed, and that from the Ethiopian word which is in turn derived from the Hebrew. *šāiṭān* is also the name of a serpent.[39]

The purely philological and etymological factor does not seem to suffice for the solution of this problem. In my opinion,

33. *Abhandlungen zur arabischen Philologie* (Leiden, 1896), p. 106; "Die Ǵinnen der Dichter," *ZDMG*, XLV, 685 ff.

34. "Aethiopische Etymologien," *ZDMG*, LXI, 615–24.

35. *Reste arabischen Heidentums* ² (1897), p. 157, n. 3.

36. *Zur Geschichte der semitischen Zischlaute*, p. 10. Unfortunately this work was not available to me.

37. *The Encyclopedia of Islam*, *s.v.* Shaiṭān (Leiden: Brill, 1934) = *Handwörterbuch d. Islam* (1941), pp. 671 ff.

38. Cf. also Lane, *An Arabic Lexicon* (London, 1863–93), *s.v.* Some of the grammarians saw in *shaiṭan* the type *faiʿāl* of *šaṭana*, while others regarded the *j* as radical, hence as the type *faʿlan* of *šāṭa*.

39. Cf. Lane, *op. cit., s.v.*

the assumption that the biblical concept penetrated into the Arabic, either directly or through Abyssinia, is more plausible than that of the reverse influence. This is in no way incompatible with a transformation of the concept corresponding to the aforementioned Arabic-pagan conceptions (plural, synonym for *ǵinn*). Satan in his final Old Testament form and especially in his Christian form is of demonic nature and could easily have been taken over by the Arabs for their own, pluralistic, form of demonism. Moreover, the plural of *śāṭān* is found already in Judaic apocryphal literature, where Satan is lord of a host of spirits, hence again appearing as split into a multiplicity, for instance in I En. 65:6 and 40:7.[40] In view of the fact that the Koran contains many elements of apocryphal Old and New Testament writings—for instance, the very Iblis concept of the Koran is derived, not from the Old Testament Satan, but from apocryphal legends of the Fallen Angel [41]—it seems to me not impossible that the pluralistic conception of Satan, also, was taken by Arabic paganism from this same source. With the extreme differentiation of late Judaic angelology and demonology, the Jewish world of religious concepts acquired a "polytheistic" feature that may have made it easily assimilable for the primitive demonism of the pre-Islamic Arabs. The name of the serpent, too, is perhaps not uninfluenced by the much earlier equation with the serpent in Paradise.[42] Enno Littmann gives positive expression to this conjecture:

> Satan, the adversary, accuser . . . is Hebrew; since the Arabic form *shaitân*, which is derived from the Abyssinian, also means "serpent," it has been conjectured that "serpent" was the original meaning of Satan; but, more probably, the Arabs learned the word in ancient times, applying it to serpents and demons of every sort, and it is

40. See also Bk. Jub. 23:29 and 50:5, quoted by Bousset-Gressmann, *op. cit.*, p. 333.

41. Koran, Suras II:32; VII:10; XV:31 f.; XVII:63; XVIII:48; XX:115; XXVIII:74 f.

42. See Wisd. of Sol. 3:24.

> only since Mohammed that it has been used again in its original sense.[43]

In any case, a reverse influence is hardly conceivable, because Satan would then appear only as a borrowed demonic being. The original Old Testament profane meaning of the Satan concept would lack any possible explanation. In view of the uncertain situation in the purely philological field, this criterion based on the Old Testament itself should decide the problem.

The exact meaning of the profane concept, its "place in life"—if I may borrow for this different context a useful phrase of Gunkel's in regard to the study of the Psalms—must be pursued with the aid of these passages, since it can be assumed that these fundamental meanings continue to play a part in the later mythological concept.

2. *The Concept of "Satan" in the Profane Realm*

In I Sam. 29:4 the princes of the Philistines turn against their king, Achish, because he wants to take David with him to fight against Saul, saying: ". . . let him [David] not go down with us to battle, lest in the battle he be an adversary [literally, *śāṭān*] to us." The same meaning of adversary in war appears in Kings. In I Kings 5:4 Solomon says in his message to Hiram: "But now Yahweh my God hath given me rest on every side, so there is neither adversary [*śāṭān*] nor evil occurrent." Then, I Kings 11:14: "And Yahweh stirred up an adversary [*śāṭān*] unto Solomon, Hadad the Edomite: he was of the king's seed in Edom." And similarly in I Kings 11:23 "And God stirred up another adversary [*śāṭān*], Rezon." Immediately following, in verse 25, it says of the same Rezon, King of Damascus: "And he was an adversary [*śāṭān*] to Israel all the days of Solomon." These passages, however, contain a deeper nuance which transcends the concrete meaning of opponent in actual warfare and already gives a subtle intimation of the future extension of the con-

43. *Morgenländische Wörter im Deutschen* [2] (1924), pp. 31–32.

cept into the metaphysical realm. This is most clearly seen in I Kings 5:4. The adversary constitutes the opposite to rest, to undisturbed peace in this life, to a condition of safe and fulfilled prosperity.[44] And the word *śāṭān* is made parallel to the "stroke of fate" (*pegaʿ rāʿ*). Apparently this connection was already held by the ancients not to be accidental. Dalman interprets *pegaʿ* as meaning, in addition to "event" and "misfortune," also "evil demon." [45] Solomon has established his kingdom and now sets out to build his temple. No foe, no "adversary" is in sight, who could cross his plans. But then God stirs up such an adversary against him, who will not let him alone as long as he lives. It is God who sends him this adversary. Here one already senses the fateful, metaphysical background behind the adversary who still appears here as a human being. Behind the profane sphere already appear flashes of the metaphysical one which breaks through completely in Num. 22:22. The concept is used with the same twofold connotation in II Sam. 19:22. There David, after his return to Jerusalem as king, turns against the sons of Zeruiah, who want to prevent him from granting Shimei his life, forfeited by his previous cursing of the king. "What have I to do with you, ye sons of Zeruiah, that ye should this day be adversaries [*śāṭān*] [46] unto me?" Here the sons of Zeruiah become "the adversary" of an inner, positive, impulse. It is tempting to assume that we already have here, in this passage, the concept of an inner adversary, which is used symbolically in reference to the sons of Zeruiah. It is therefore understandable that the Zürich Bible here translates Satan by "tempter."

44. Compare also Karl Marti, "Zwei Studien zu Sacharja," *Theologische Studien und Kritiken* (1892), pp. 217 f., on these passages: "Therefore those also who oppose themselves to the quiet and undisturbed governing and the peaceful development of a state are called Satan. . . ."

45. *Aramäisch-Neuhebräisches Wörterbuch, s.v.* According to Förster, in his article "δαίμων" in Kittel, *Theol. Wörterbuch zum Neuen Testament* (1933), p. 13, *pegaʿ*, in Tannaitic Judaism = "the attacker" (rare).

46. The Zürich Bible here translates "Satan" as "tempter." See the remarks which follow.

Luther in this passage writes "Satan," thereby presumably taking the same position; that is, he had in mind the fully formed figure of Satan, used as an image for the men opposing David. However, it seems to me questionable whether, in this relatively old text, such an interpretation and a corresponding translation is possible. It presupposes not only the figure of Satan, who appears only later in the Old Testament, but even the still later conception of late Judaism—which went beyond the Old Testament—of Satan as the evil drive (*yeṣer hā-rā'*) in the human soul. Could not this passage also be explained in the sense of an inimical attitude, an opposition, a contradiction, of David's intention of letting justice give way to mercy in the case of Shimei? All the more so since the same situation is already presented in II Sam. 16:10 ff., where David is fleeing before Absalom. Here, too, David resists the demand of the sons of Zeruiah to slay Shimei, who has cursed him, with the words: "What have I to do with you, ye sons of Zeruiah?" (without the additional phrase of II Sam. 19:22, "that ye should this day be Satan to me"). He simply separates himself from the standpoint of the sons of Zeruiah and withdraws into his own inner, independent attitude, which shows a remarkable magnanimity:

> so let him curse, because Yahweh hath said unto him, Curse David. Who shall then say, Wherefore hast thou done so? And David said to Abishai, and to all his servants, Behold, my son, which came forth from my bowels, seeketh my life; how much more now may this Benjamite do it? Let him alone, and let him curse, for Yahweh hath bidden him. It may be that Yahweh will look on mine affliction, and that Yahweh will requite me good for his cursing this day.

And most impressively it continues:

> And as David and his men went by the way, Shimei went along on the hill's side over against him, and cursed as he went, and threw stones at him, and cast dust. And the king, and all the people that were with him, came weary [to the Jordan] and refreshed themselves there.

Such a magnanimous attitude cannot always be taken for granted, even for a David. It would have been very possible for David to regress to a "more normal" need for revenge when, in II Sam. 19:22, he returned to Jerusalem as reinstated rightful king, and Shimei came to beg forgiveness for his iniquity. The standpoint of Zeruiah's sons might now have been even more of a temptation, and this time he does not forgive as a humble human being standing before God alone but as a great-hearted king who bestows amnesty to celebrate his return. "What have I to do with you, ye sons of Zeruiah, that ye should this day be adversaries [*śāṭān*] unto me? shall there any man be put to death this day in Israel? for do not I know that I am this day king over Israel?"

Thus, even though in my opinion one cannot think here of the later meaning of Satan as "tempter," this passage, too, nevertheless goes beyond the external, concrete opposition of Satan as enemy, insofar as the opposition is met on the psychic plane and is expressed in the image of the outer foe. The profane concept of Satan comes to be an image of an *inner* opposition. However, such an interpretation does not as yet presuppose the mythological Satan figure.[47]

47. Cf. also Henry Preserved Smith, *The Book of Samuel* ("International Critical Commentary" series) (1912), pp. 363 f.: "David again disclaims fellowship with the sons of Zeruiah who would be his *adversary*, hindering him from doing what he would. *Today a man shall be put to death in Israel?* Evidently conciliation was to be the order of the day, for the king had the confidence that he was fully restored to his throne. The acclaim of the people has moved him to this generosity." And further (p. 364): " . . . the Philistines contemplated the possibility of David's becoming a satan, *a traitor* in the *camp:* in much the same light David views the sons of Zeruiah here." The word *śāṭān* here is also taken as a profane concept by Karl Marti ("Zwei Studien zu Sacharja," p. 218); and by Caspari in his commentary on The Books of Samuel (*Sellin-Kommentar*, p. 595, n. 4). Kaupel, too (*Die Dämonen des Alten Testaments* [1930], p. 123), sees that a human adversary is meant here, but tries, though hesitatingly, to bring Satan into the old text as a metaphysical entity by remarking on the above passage: "Might one not now and then, when calling an adversary *śāṭān*, wish to make a tacit comparison between the supernatural adversary of man, as well as of God, and the immediate opponent?" This corresponds to his general view, for which there is no evidence in the text, that in the Old

It is a quite different story if we consider this passage as a profane parallel to the judgment scene at the divine court in Zechariah's vision, chapter 3:1 ff. Here it is to some extent a conflict in the divine realm, in heaven: the *mal'āk Yahweh* proclaims mercy and commands Satan—who is clamoring for justice and the punishment of Joshua, the high priest—to be silent, just as David commands silence of the sons of Zeruiah. To this extent, here, too, the metaphysical background becomes visible. Behind the moral conflict of man there stands in reality the divine conflict, the judgment in heaven. It is also a fine example of what I tried to make clear in the Introduction about the relation between God and the human soul. What happens in David's soul and in his actual situation is somehow a reflection of what is happening in the divine sphere. But as yet these are two streams that do not meet, are not united in a conscious mind. David experiences this divine drama in himself, but does not yet know its divine character.

3. *The Concept of "Satan" in the Metaphysical Realm*

THE DIVINE and the human planes meet for the first time in a most significant way in Num. 22:22. Here it is an *angel* who stands in the way of Balaam, the *human being*, as *śāṭān*, as adversary. He is by no means as yet the demonic figure called "Satan," but the *mal'āk Yahweh,* who blocks Balaam's path, *le-śāṭān-lō,* "for an adversary to him." The term *śāṭān* is used here only in apposition to *mal'āk Yahweh:* he stands in Balaam's way as adversary.

The Balaam passage, as it relates to the development of the Satan figure, will be discussed in more detail later (see pp. 72 ff.). Here it is only important to establish the fact that a divine being stands as "adversary" in the way of a human being. That which crosses human plans and wishes comes from the divine sphere; that is, the human experience of this

---

Testament Satan was already the archenemy of God and man (see above, p. 11).

world has expanded in human consciousness to a metaphysical experience. The "resistance" comes ultimately from God. But Satan is not yet a mythological figure; *śāṭān* is, as in the preceding passages, a *functional concept,* not a proper name.

The story told in Job 1:6 ff. and 2:1 ff. represents a further step in this development. Again, as in Num. 22:22, it is a matter of the divine realm. Here, too, the adversary is an angel, one of the *benē-hā-'elōhīm,* the sons of God, or divine beings. What is new, however, is that the adversary is not merely God's messenger; he stands over against God in a dialectical relation. Here he has become a personal figure in the divine realm, but here, too, he is the personification of a divine *function.*

Differing in content, yet the same in form, we find the concept of Satan in Zech. 3:1 ff. Here again Satan stands opposite God, i.e., the *mal'āk Yahweh.* Thus, it is not a personality essentially differentiated from Yahweh who confronts the *mal'āk Yahweh,* but rather two aspects of God who confront each other.

In only one Satan passage of the Old Testament—the latest one—in I Chron. 21:1, the word *śāṭān* appears without an article as a proper name. There it is said: "And Satan stood up against Israel, and provoked David to number Israel." This passage receives great theological significance because of its correspondence to II Sam. 24:1, where it says: "And again the *anger of Yahweh* was kindled against Israel, and he moved David against them saying, Go, number Israel and Judah." Here Satan is an independent personality, who in a particular function appears instead of God. Torczyner's translation, "And *a satan* stood up against Israel," [48] seems to me for this reason incorrect. The close correspondence to II Sam. 24:1 demands an equally *defined* personality, aside from the fact that such indefiniteness would leave the sentence theologically hanging in the air. Who is this "one" adversary from the divine realm supposed to be, since there is nowhere else any mention of a plurality of such satans? The term can refer

48. "How Satan Came into the World," p. 18.

only to the figure which alone has been mentioned so far, the hypostatized divine function of "opposition" which has become an independent personality.[49]

From what has been said so far it is not difficult to see the evidence for a further development of the personified function into the independent personality "Satan." Theologically, however, it cannot be ignored that it is just through the exchange of the divine persons that their intrinsic identity becomes especially clear. Satan does nothing other than what God himself does in other contexts. This will be discussed more closely later.

The result of our research in regard to the name "Satan" can be summarized as follows:

Śāṭān is a *functional* concept which has its root in the meaning of the verb "to oppose inimically" and which in a few passages appears as *nomen appelativum* with a profane meaning; in other, exclusively later passages, it occurs as a mythological figure. The passage in Numbers where the concept *śāṭān* appears in the divine realm, but not yet as a mythological figure, represents a bridge between the profane and mythological meanings. As the *nomen proprium* of an independent demon standing opposed to God, the concept appears in only one, and that the latest passage: I Chron. 21:1.

From this we can already draw a fundamental conclusion concerning the nature of Satan. He is no demonic residue from pre-Yahwistic time who, as such, leads a more or less degraded, shadowy existence beside Yahweh. Karl Marti, too, is of the opinion that Satan cannot be subsumed among the old demons, "for Satan looks rather strange in the midst of the *Seʿîrîm* . . . , the ghostly figures that tussle about all over the wilderness. In their circle, he is an alien figure, not only by the way he appears in Zechariah, but also by his name." [50] A comparison with other remnants of this sort from

49. On the views of Kaupel and Kugler, according to whom it is not a demon but a human enemy of David's who incites him to count the people, see below, p. 155, n. 14.

50. K. Marti, "Zwei Studien zu Sacharja," p. 227.

pre-Yahwistic religions will serve to support this statement.

The first thing that strikes us is that these other figures are designated by names or generic concepts which for the most part denote their foreign origin.

In the case of Azazel, the desert demon in Leviticus 16:8, 10, 26 (RSV), who presents the closest analogy to Satan, the etymology is uncertain. The theory of the Jewish exegesists (Targum, Raschi, Pseudojonathan, Kimchi), according to which Azazel is the name of a place in the desert, rules itself out, since its juxtaposition to the name of Yahweh obviously points to a personal being.[51] Hans Duhm [52] refers to the frequently advanced [53] idea that Azazel derives from *'āzal* and is to be translated by "completely doing away with." This theory is based on the translation of LXX: ἀποπομπαῖος.[54] A similar etymology is advanced by Robert Eisler.[55] He translates *'azā'zēl* with "off-going, departing male goat" (*'az* = *'ēz*), corresponding to Symmacho's Greek translation: τράγος ἀπολυόμενος. The principal objection to this interpretation is that in Leviticus 16 it is not the scapegoat sent into the wilderness that bears the name Azazel, but a being of the wilderness to whom the goat is sent. In disagreement with Eisler, I do not believe that the supposition of a wilderness demon can be avoided. The derivation from *'āzāz* and *'ēl*, referred to by Roskoff,[56] seems to me more plausible and to offer clues toward a more comprehensive meaning. In that

51. See Benzinger, "Azazel," *Encyclopaedia Biblica;* cf. also on the passage *HSAT* [4]; Roskoff, *Geschichte des Teufels* (1869), I, 179; Alfred Bertholet, "Leviticus," *Marti-Handkommentar z. A.T.* (1901).

52. "Die bösen Geister im Alten Testament" (diss., Tübingen, 1904), p. 56.

53. Among others by Merx, *Bibl. Lex.*, I, 256 (see *Encycl. Bibl.*, "Azazel," p. 395); also William Caldwell, "The Doctrine of Satan," *Biblical World*, XLI (1913), 30; and George A. Barton, "Demons and Spirits," *Encyclopedia of Religion and Ethics* (13 vols.), ed. James Hastings (1925).

54. According to Roskoff, *op. cit.*, I, 179, it goes back to H. Ewald (*Kritische Grammatik*, p. 243; *Ausführliches Lehrbuch der hebräischen Sprache*, 6th ed., § 158c).

55. *Arch. f. Religionswissenschaft*, XXVII (1929), 177 ff.

56. *Op. cit.*, I, 183.

case *'azā'zēl* would mean "the strong one of God." In support of this Roskoff cites Fürst[57] and Diestel,[58] who adduce a number of names of divinities which are formed with *'azīz.* Above all, there is a Phoenician god, *'azīz,* to whom the powerful effects of the sun are ascribed. This would, by the way, suffice to explain the desert character of Azazel without having to go back directly to Seth, to whom sacrifices of atonement were brought. It is conceivable that this Phoenician god had already assimilated traits of Seth, in view of the close connection between Egypt and Canaan in the Amarna Period, especially since the designation Seth-Zaphon for the Syrian god Baal-Zaphon has been found on an excavated stele of that period (around 1300 B.C.).[59] In any case, to restrict this figure completely to Egyptian influence, as Roskoff does, leaves the Semitic name unexplained. Further, there also occurs the name of a god, *bēl-'azīz,* "Bel the Strong"; then there is the promontory, Marti Rusaziz, i.e., *rōš-'azīz,* "The Head of the Strong One," on the Punic Coast; the Mars of Edessa is called Ἄζιζος = "the Strong One, the Powerful One." Baudissin thinks it possible that a foreign god with this name may have changed into a demon.[60] Gesenius-Buhl also voices the conjecture that there has been a merging of *'āzāz* and *'ēl.* But its meaning is considered unknown.[61] Further literature is found in Koehler-Baumgartner;[62] they, however, do not consider plausible any of the derivations they mention. But for our context it is of essential importance that we deal

57. *Hebr.-chald. Handwörterbuch, s. v.* "Azazel."

58. "Set-Typhon, Asahel und Satan," *Zeitschrift für die historische Theologie,* XXX (1860), No. 2. For further discussion of this article, see below, pp. 83 ff.

59. See G. Seippel, *Der Typhonmythus* (1939), p. 20.

60. Baudissin, *Studien zur Semitischen Religionsgeschichte,* I, 141.

61. To enter into more of the literature cited there in regard to the name Azazel would lead us too far in this context.

62. *Lexikon, s.v.* From these references I would like to mention only Hubert Grimme ("Das Alter des israelitischen Versöhnungstages," *Archiv für Religionswissenschaft,* XIV, 1911), whose conception differs in principle from those mentioned above. According to him, "*'azā'zēl*" means "the little hairy one," and stems from a word occurring in Ethiopian: *g^{u}ezag^{u}ez* = "shaggy fleece."

with a demon of foreign origin and that, in the opinion of the majority, *'azā'zēl* represents a proper name.

In the case of *Lilith,* the Babylonian origin is beyond doubt (Isa. 34:14). Gesenius-Buhl and Koehler-Baumgartner refer to the Akkadian *lilu,* from *lilitu* = "evil demon." [63]

For *Leviathan,* the cosmic dragon-beast in Job 3:8 (RSV) and elsewhere,[64] Koehler-Baumgartner in addition to the derivation from the Hebrew *liwjā* = "wound," [65] adduce a reference to the Egyptian *ltn.*[66]

Behemoth, the name of a hippopotamus-like monster (Job 40:15) is considered by many to be of Egyptian origin. Budde [67] believes with Spiegelberg that Jablonski's derivation from the Egyptian *p-ehe-moû* ("water buffalo") is correct.[68] Others, among them Cheyne [69] and W. Max Müller,[70] disagree with this opinion.

As for *Rahab,* derived from the Akkadian *ra'abu, raḫabu* ("to be tempestuous"),[71] Gunkel and others assume a Babylonian origin.[72] According to Gunkel she is the "personification

63. According to Lenormant (*La Magie chez les Chaldéens,* p. 36; *cit.* Duhm, *op. cit.,* p. 51), *lil* and *lilit* mean "incubus" and "succubus," and derive from the Babylonian *lilâtu* = "evening." According to Gesenius-Buhl, however, Lilith became thought of as a night demon only through folk etymology. Cf. also Bruno Meissner, *Babylonien und Assyrien,* (1925), II, 201: *Lîlîtu* forms with *Lîlû* and the "maid of *Lîlû*" (*Ardat Lîlî*) a triad. "Originally they were probably storm demons who, however, as the result of a false etymology were finally thought of as night spirits."

64. Pss. 74:14; 104:26.

65. See also Gesenius-Buhl. Gunkel gives the derivation: *liwyā* = "wreath"; *liwyātān* = "the wreath-like," i.e., the ocean, "which winds its girdle of waves around the lands" (*Schöpfung und Chaos* [Göttingen, 1895], p. 46).

66. W. Baumgartner (*Theol. Rundschau* [1941], p. 162) mentions that *ltn* already exists in Ugaritic. Cf. also G. Seippel, *op. cit.,* p. 137.

67. Karl Budde, *Das Buch Hiob* ("Göttinger Handkommentar zum Alten Testament") (1913), p. 257.

68. Mentioned in Koehler-Baumgartner, *Lexikon.*

69. *Encyclopaedia Biblica,* ed. T. K. Cheyne and J. S. Black (1899–1907), I, 519 (*cit.* Budde, *op. cit.,* p. 257).

70. Gesenius-Buhl, *s.v.*

71. See Koehler-Baumgartner and Gesenius-Buhl, *s.v.*

72. Gunkel, *op. cit.,* pp. 30 ff.

of *tehōm*, of chaos." [73] He mentions further that in one of the numerous variants of the Tiamat myth, Tiamat bears the name of *ribbu* (= *ribhu* =*rahab*), a reading, however, which is not fully established.[74]

The cherubim are also probably of Babylonian origin.[75] According to Gesenius,[76] the bull *colossi* are called *Karibâti*, "the blessing ones," [77] in Assyrian inscriptions from Susa. In other Assyrian inscriptions they are called *Kuribi* (from the same Assyrian root *karābu*, "to bless").[78]

For the seraphim (Isa. 6:2, 6; probably from the Akkadian *šarāpu*, "to kindle, to burn up") there has been substantiated, along with the usual association with Šarrapu-Nergal,[79] an Egyptian provenance: late Egyptian *srrf*, "dragon, griffin, serpent." [80]

Firmly established is the Babylonian origin of the *šēdīm* (Deut. 32:17; Ps. 106:37). According to Zimmern and others it is probably derived from the Assyrian *šēdu* = "bull-god, good and evil demon." [81]

The name of the *śeʿīrīm*, the goat demons, is Hebrew, from *śāʿīr*, "the hairy one, the he-goat." However, from the context in which they appear, they are characterized as having been, to begin with, exclusively demonic beings. In Isa. 13:21 they are dancing satyrs; in Isa. 34:14 they people the desert, where Lilith also dwells. The wilderness was already in the Babylonian conception the abiding-place of demons. This is

73. *Ibid.*, p. 32.
74. *Ibid.*, p. 29.
75. Gesenius-Buhl and Koehler-Baumgartner, *s.v.*
76. *Hebr. u. aramäisches Wörterbuch*, 14th ed., *cit.* in regard to Gen. 3:24 by Gunkel, *Genesis* (4th ed., 1917), p. 25.
77. For further literature see Koehler-Baumgartner and Gesenius-Buhl, *s.v.*
78. Robert H. Pfeiffer, *Journal of Biblical Literature*, XLI (1922), 249 f.
79. In opposition to Zimmern, *KAT*, 415; see Gesenius-Buhl, *s.v.*
80. Gesenius-Buhl, *s.v.* According to Spiegelberg (*Der aegyptische Mythos vom Sonnenauge* [1917], p. 39), from the demotic *srrf*, Egyptian *srf* = "to be warm" (Koehler-Baumgartner, *s.v.*).
81. According to Koehler-Baumgartner (referring to *ZAW*, LIV, 291 f.), from *jāšūd*, Ar. *iswadda* = "to be black."

shown by the following incantation against the evil Alû: [82]

> Evil Alû, go to the desert place!
> . . . .
> Your dwelling is a destroyed ruin. . . .

The listing-together of wild beasts and demons as desert inhabitants in Isaiah, to which Kaupel refers,[83] finds an analogy among the Arabs, who also think of the *ǵinns* as being closely connected to the wild animals. In Lev. 17:7 it is forbidden to sacrifice to the *śe'īrīm;* and in II Chron. 11:15 they appear with the calves as images in the idol worship of Jeroboam. Baudissin is therefore presumably justified in calling them a "residue of ancient Hebrew paganism." [84]

All these residues of pre-Yahwistic religion have either remained outside the Yahweh religion, like the *šēdīm, śe'īrīm,* and Lilith, or they have been included as his attributes in the personality of Yahweh, like the seraphim and cherubim who stand about him in Isaiah 6 (see also below, p. 105), or Behemoth and Leviathan, who appear in the Book of Job (chapter 40) as symbolic images of his nature.

Azazel seems to be an exception; he belongs to the cult and is at the same time opposite Yahweh. This demonic figure therefore deserves special attention in our connection, because its opposition (in my opinion only apparent) to Yahweh has led many scholars to see him as identical to the Old Testament Satan [85] or as a previous form of him.[86] Aside from

82. Ungnad, *Die Religion der Babylonier und Assyrer* (1921), p. 290.
83. Kaupel, *Die Dämonen des Alten Testaments* (1930), p. 10; in opposition to the opinion of W. R. Smith (*Religion of the Semites* [1956], p. 120), who for this reason holds all the animals mentioned there to be demons.
84. *Op. cit.*, p. 137.
85. Galling (*RGG* ² [1928], II, 964) says: "He is, as the receiver of sins, a sort of opponent of God, a figure corresponding to Satan." In this he is followed by Kaupel (*op. cit.*, p. 91). The identification of Azazel and Satan and Serpent in Genesis 3 is already found in Origen (see Caldwell, n. 53, above).
86. Benzinger (*op. cit.*, p. 395) accepts Reuss's assumption that "the conception of Azāzel lies on the way which led later to that of the

the indication of the proper name which shows Azazel, in contrast to Satan, to have been a demon from of old, it must be considered that we obviously have to do here with an ancient ritual. This view is supported by Driver: "No doubt the ritual is a survival from another stage of popular belief, engrafted on and accommodated to the sacrificial system of the Hebrews. . . ." [87] Referring to Frazer [88] he draws attention to the primitive character of the ritual, which has many analogies in the Old Testament itself (Lev. 14:4 ff., 49 ff.) and in other countries.[89] Further indication of the great age of the ritual is advanced by Max Loehr.[90]

> Asasel, the Holy Tabernacle, above all the "camp" of Israel, are signs seeming to point back to the period before the settling in Canaan, to an existence in the shepherd steppes of southernmost Palestine. Perhaps the sending of a goat to Asasel is a pre-Mosaic ritual of atonement of one of the Lea tribes, which for some unknown reasons was adopted into the cult of Yahweh when Yahwism arose.

A close examination of the obviously ancient ritual shows a peculiarity which proves to be decisive with regard to our question: The demon Azazel does not appear as an opponent to Yahweh, as a power which really stands in opposition to him. This is shown above all by the fact, already pointed out by Justinus [91] and emphasized by Roskoff [92] and most other modern scholars,[93] that Leviticus 16 does not relate to a

---

devil" (*Geschichte der Heiligen Schriften des Alten Testaments* [1890], p. 501). Cf. also Roskoff, *op. cit.*, p. 197; see above, p. 8, n. 15.

87. Art. "Azazel," *Dictionary of the Bible* (1923), I, 207 f.

88. *Golden Bough*, 3d ed. (1919), II, 182 ff.; see also H. Grimme, *op. cit.*

89. *Dictionary of the Bible, s.v.* "Azazel."

90. "Das Ritual von Lev. 16. Untersuchungen zum Hexateuchproblem III," *Schriften der Königsberger Gelehrten Gesellschaft* (1925), p. 11.

91. *Dialog mit Tryphon 40*, p. 4; *cit.* Kaupel, *op. cit.*, p. 87.

92. *Op. cit.*, p. 186.

93. Among others, J. Gutmann, "Asasel," *Encycl. Judaica;* Eichrodt, *Theologie des A.T.* (1906), II, 120; B. Stade, *Theologie des A.T.*

sacrifice. In my opinion, Roskoff's view can be largely followed:

> Azazel is not a power to whom a sacrifice would be offered in atonement, and the dualism which suggests itself through him is only shadowy. He is merely the qualification of abstract impurity as against the absolute purity of Yahweh; he is only a shadow image without reality against the solely real power of Yahweh.[94]

The Azazel ritual seems to me to offer a unique insight into a definite phase in the development of the monotheistic concept of God, a "snapshot" of the process of repressing the ancient demonic deities. In a way it catches a picture of the repression process itself. Azazel, originally probably an ancient demonic deity (see above, pp. 41 ff.), is now nothing more than a concept, still extant as such, but largely hollowed out. He is no more than a symbol of the desert.[95] He is banished to the place where there is no more life. The opposite of the desolate Azazel wilderness is the "Holy Tabernacle," the dwelling-place of the Living God. Corresponding on the human plane to God's becoming a *holy* God is the demand on men for sanctification. Hence, within the psyche, too, there is a splitting-off corresponding to the divine process. If one looks at the human side of the ritual psychologically, the he-goat can serve very well as the symbol of the animal libido in the human being. This force is split; there are now two goats. One must be sacrificed to Yahweh, and the other must disappear into the wilderness. The lot decides which is meant for Yahweh and which for Azazel. Hence, as such they are

---

(1906), I, 188 ff.; E. Kautzsch, *Bibl. Theologie des A.T.* (1911), pp. 20, 347; G. Hölscher, *Geschichte der israelitisch-jüdischen Religion* (1922), §9, 9.

94. *Op. cit.*, p. 186.

95. Compare to the passage *HSAT* [4], p. 185, note c: "The sending out of Azazel, who is laden with the sin of the people, must be considered as simply the symbolic removal of sin and impurity from the land holy to Jahwe to the realm of the impure and the unholy."

identical. It is the same instinctual energy which must be in part sacrificed to Yahweh and in part done away with. So only a portion of the libido is sublimated; the other is rejected as sin, is repressed. The sinful libido goes back to its "origin," into the wilderness; that is, it sinks into the unconscious, which, because of the splitting-off, has the character of wilderness. The unconscious is burdened with the sin. So, in a later period, when Azazel again achieved significance as a demon, a Midrash says: "The sins are sent to Azazel, *so that he may carry them.*" [96]

Psychologically, though on another plane, what happens in the Azazel ritual is similar to what happens in Zechariah's vision of the woman in the ephah (5:11).[97] Here, as there, the sin is pushed away, to a place identified with it: in the early period, to the wilderness; later, to the heathen Babylon.

Leonard Rost offers a study on the concept *riš'ā.*[98] Although he admits "that the meaning of the rare expression *riš'ah* is established in other passages only in a wider, not in the older purely forensic sense," [99] he nevertheless applies the latter interpretation to Zech. 5:8. According to this, *riš'ā* is the condemnation to exile. He finds the continued use of the curse in Haggai and hinted at in Zech. 8:10 ff., in the failure of the crops: "The empty granary, into which the personified sentence of judgment has entered, departs from the land." The sentence of condemnation is then carried to Babylon, the seat of the oppressive power, in the empty ephah which characterizes the failure of the crop. I cannot subscribe to Rost's conclusions. They are contradicted, above all, by earlier evidence for the meaning "wickedness, godlessness," as,

96. Midrash Abchir (Jalkut Gen. §44), *cit.* Gruenbaum, "Beiträge zur vergleichenden Mythologie aus der Hagada," *ZDMG,* XXXI (1877), 226 (italics added).

97. The comparison between the two passages is drawn, among others, by Benzinger, "Asasel," *Encycl. Biblica,* p. 395; J. Gutmann, "Asasel," *Encycl. Judaica;* Eichrodt, *Theologie des A.T.*, II, 120.

98. "Erwägungen zu Sacharjas 7. Nachtgesicht," *ZAW,* LVII–LVIII (1939–41), 224 ff.

99. *Ibid.*, p. 226.

for instance, in Isa. 9:18: "For wickedness [*riš'ā*] burneth as the fire," and Ezek. 18:27: "Again, when the wicked man turneth away from his wickedness [*ū-bešūb rāšā' mēriš'ātō*]." Here a translation in the forensic sense as "pronouncement of judgment" is quite impossible (aside from the immediately following parallel use of *peša'*). A comparison should also be made with Mal. 1:4, where Edom is called the "border of wickedness" (*gebūl riš'ā*), which gives a very close parallel to our passage, where the *riš'ā* is carried to Babylon as its permanent abiding-place. Least of all is there any explanation in Rost's thesis for the personification of the *riš'ā* as a woman.

It seems very significant for our context that in Zechariah a woman should appear as the incarnation of sin. Woman is by nature closer to the earth and to the darkness of the unconscious. This is shown most markedly in the Chinese Yang-Yin polarity, as it is presented, for example, in one of the oldest books, the *I Ching*, or "Book of Changes."[100] The Yahweh religion, more masculine in character, represents, as it were, the ascent of consciousness from the maternal primal womb of the nature religions. This shows, for example, in the symbolic content of the revelation on Sinai after the liberation from Egyptian bondage. In the Old Testament, Egypt is frequently identified with Rahab, which points up its symbolic feminine quality, in contrast to which the light-theophany on Sinai can mean literally "illumination," the beginning of consciousness. We may think also of the image of Yahweh overcoming Rahab, which has its prototype in Marduk's battle with Tiamat. In this masculine religion, woman could, even necessarily must, become the symbol of the "sinful" libido detached from Yahweh. Looked at from the point of view of the history of ideas, it seems to me that even in the Old Testament a connection is hinted at between woman and Azazel and Satan, which later led to an identification of the two figures in the Apocrypha. Even if it is false to speak also of a *genetic* identity of

100. *The I Ching or Book of Changes,* trans. Richard Wilhelm, rendered into English by Cary F. Baynes (1950).

Satan with the Paradise serpent (see above, p. 11, n. 25), there still exists a connection of nature between them, as will be shown later (see below, p. 131). Just as Eve makes a pact with the serpent against God, so, unconsciously, Job's wife shows herself on the side of Satan (see below, p. 113). Not until a later time had the process of differentiation led to a separation of the different sides of the Godhead, thus effecting a revitalization of pre-Yahwistic demons in the form of good and bad angels. Eric Stave [101] speaks of the fact that in these evil powers "a residue of the nature religion repressed by the preaching of the prophets, to be sure under the influence of a different religious conception, was awakened to new life, as it were." Thus, the development went, so to speak, in the direction of a new polytheistization of Yahwism, on a higher level. Only in this time did Azazel become one of the fallen angels in the Book of Enoch, and interchangeable with Satan. The same process is shown by the fact that *maśṭēmā*, in Hos. 9:7 (see above, pp. 27 f.), became a name of Satan in the Book of Jubilees. Such a developmental phenomenon is more probable here than a mere misinterpretation of the name, as Gunkel assumes.[102] The connection, still hidden in the Old Testament, between Satan and woman, on the one hand, and the Azazel ritual and Zechariah's woman in the ephah, on the other, comes clearly to the surface in the Book of Enoch: Azazel-Satan seduces the women to sin by teaching them how to make cosmetics. Here (through the parallel to Genesis 6, where the sons of God unite with the daughters of men) the relation between women and Satan is implied, since in the Book of Job Satan is also one of the sons of God (see below, pp. 98 ff.).

From all this it should become clear that Azazel and Satan, who were identified in postbiblical times, have nothing to do with each other genetically. Thus, Azazel does not change anything in the picture concerning a definite discrimination

101. *Ueber den Einfluss des Parsismus auf das Judentum* (Haarlem, 1898), p. 269.

102. "Teufelsglaube," *RGG* ², V, 1062.

between the Satan figure in the Old Testament and pre-Yahwistic demons.

The following points can now be established with respect to Satan, as against all those residues from other religions which have been discussed.

1. He had no proper name to begin with, but is called by a Hebrew *nomen appellativum,* which only in the latest passage becomes a proper name. Moreover, it is a *nomen appellativum* which, as such, does not designate demonic beings, like the *šēdīm,* for example, but also occurs in regard to the profane realm. In the case of the *śe'īrīm*—a term which verbally is analogous to "Satan" insofar as this concept is also used partly in the profane sense (ordinary goats) and partly in the demonic meaning—the context in which it is used has decisive weight; the *śe'īrīm* appear together with other pre-Yahwistic demons and so belong to a category of appearances which are expressly opposed to Yahwism and are combated by it.

2. Satan, in contrast to the real cacodemons, belongs to the divine realm. And in contrast to the mythological figures of the seraphim, the cherubim, Leviathan, and Behemoth, he does not represent the nature side of God (witness their animal shapes!) but is a *spiritual* demon who stands in a dialectical confrontation with God (see below, pp. 104 ff.). The animal attributes (horns, goat's feet, tail) "grew" on him only later. C. G. Jung writes about this:

> The Church has the doctrine of the devil, of an evil principle, whom we like to imagine complete with cloven hoofs, horns, and tail, half man, half beast, a chthonic deity apparently escaped from the rout of Dionysus, the sole surviving champion of the sinful joys of paganism. An excellent picture, and one which exactly describes the grotesque and sinister side of the unconscious; for we have never really come to grips with it and consequently it has remained in its original savage state.[103]

103. C. G. Jung, "Psychology of the Transference," *The Practice of Psychotherapy,* in *Collected Works* (Bollingen Series XX), XVI, 191.

The Old Testament Satan, however, is still a personified function of God, which, as we shall see, develops step by step and detaches itself from the divine personality. Seen from this angle, Hans Duhm's basic error in simply including Satan among the cacodemons is again made visible in its whole import. His purely external classification, as has already been mentioned, misses the essential point. Satan is in no way understood as the important theological phenomenon which he represents.

This implies at the same time that he is also not a concept adopted from a foreign religion. It does not by any means exclude the question of whether traits of alien neighboring gods may adhere to his *image*. But such an influence could find adequate expression only through an *inner-divine* process within the Yahweh religion itself. Religious figures are not simply adopted; they correspond to a need which as yet lacks expression. Otherwise there would be no explanation of why such an influence, say the Babylonian, had not made itself felt much earlier or to a much greater extent. Only when the Satan figure was ripe enough to detach itself from the personality of God could traits of similar figures in the religious environment become associated with it.[104] This problem will be pursued in detail later (see below, pp. 133 ff.).

First, however, we must corroborate in detail what we have learned from the analysis of the names and concepts and must delineate and complete the image of Satan in its further characteristics.

104. Cf. Gerhard von Rad, "Eschatologische Erwägungen zu den Königspsalmen," *ZAW*, LVIII (1940–41), 219: "If Yahwism includes in its conceptual world something originally foreign to it, the premises for this must have already existed within itself." Von Rad shows this beautifully through the example of the King-Psalms, whose form, borrowed from the Oriental court style, became a vessel for its own content, the Messianic kingdom. Compare also Förster's article "δαιμων," in Kittel, *Theol. Wörterbuch zum Neuen Testament*, which emphasizes for the later time also "that Judaism has adopted nothing for which the ground had not already been prepared within itself" (p. 16).

The immediate question is: In *what forms* of divine manifestation does Satan appear, and what do they signify? We will return to the story of Balaam, as the first Old Testament passage where the Satanic function appears in the divine realm.

The *mal'āk Yahweh* as Satan in the Story of Balaam (Numbers 22:22 ff.)

THE INTERMEDIATE POSITION of this story in the development of the Satan concept has already been pointed out. Here *śāṭān* is not yet the designation of, or even the proper name of, a mythological person, but the concept is already applied to a familiar mythological figure, the *mal'āk Yahweh,* defining more closely one of its qualities. The concept has here a meaning entirely and exclusively derived from the profane realm; it is "enemy, adversary," without further differentiation of this inimical quality into "accuser," as in Job and Zechariah, or as "provoker," as in I Chron. 21:1. Yet, what makes the Numbers passage significant is that this function from the profane sphere is met with for the first time in the divine sphere. Num. 22:22 is, in a way, the point of intersection, where the profane and the divine phenomena cross; or, to use another image, the place where the profane concept changes into the mythological concept. *Śāṭān,* adversary, is here a quality of the *mal'āk Yahweh.* Hence, the transition of the Satan concept from the human to the divine realm is shown in the *mal'āk Yahweh.* It is true that Hans Duhm refers to this passage,[1] but only among the "profane" examples of Solomon and David, without consideration of the significant "changes of scene" from the human to the divine

1. Hans Duhm, "Die bösen Geister im Alten Testament" (diss., Tübingen, 1904), p. 16.

realm. From our point of view, however, this passage is most elucidating and significant. It demands of us nothing less than the understanding of the Satan concept in relation to that of the *mal'āk Yahweh.*

1. *Occurrence and Theological Significance of the* mal'āk Yahweh *in the Old Testament*

Mal'āk is a Hebrew nominal form, occurring also in Phoenician; i.e., in Ugaritic, "an ancient Canaanite dialect of the second millennium B.C. which is closely related to Phoenician." [2] It derives from the stem *l'āk,* which cannot be traced in Hebrew; Arabic *la'aka,* "to send on a commission." [3] *Mal'āk Yahweh* is therefore "the emissary of God." It is important in our context that he carries out functions which in other passages, often even in the same story, are assumed by Yahweh himself. For instance, in Gen. 16:10, the *mal'āk Yahweh* says to Hagar: "I will multiply thy seed exceedingly. . . ." [4] Here he makes a promise which in another passage (Gen. 15:5) is given by Yahweh himself. In Exod. 3:2 the *mal'āk Yahweh* appears to Moses in a thorn bush, but in verse 4 it is Yahweh himself who speaks to Moses from the bush. In Jacob's dream (Gen. 31:13) the *mal'āk Yahweh* expressly states his identity with Yahweh: "I am the God of Bethel, where thou anointedst the pillar, and where thou vowedst a vow unto me." Equally clearly he identifies himself with Yahweh in Judg. 2:1–3: "And the *mal'āk Yahweh* . . . said, I made you to go up out of Egypt, and have brought you unto the land which I sware unto your fathers. . . ." Just as in Exod. 13:21 Yahweh goes before Israel as a pillar of cloud, so does the *mal'āk Yahweh* in Exod. 14:19. Immediately

2. W. Baumgartner, "Zum Problem des 'Jahwe-Engels,'" *Schweiz. Theol. Umschau* (14th year, Oct., 1944), No. 5.

3. See Gerhard von Rad, art. "ἄγγελος," in Kittel, *Theologisches Wörterbuch zum Neuen Testament,* I, 75–79. See also Gesenius-Buhl, *Hebr. und aram. Handwörterbuch über das Alte Testament* (1915), *s.v.,* and Koehler-Baumgartner, *Lexikon in veteris testamenti libros* (Leiden: Brill, 1958), *s.v.*

4. See also Gen. 21:18.

following, in Exod. 14:24, it is again Yahweh himself who at the time of the morning watch "looked unto the host of the Egyptians through the pillar of fire and the cloud and troubled the host of the Egyptians." Yahweh and his angel also show identical behavior in other passages. Just as in Gen. 32:29 Elohim, who wrestles with Jacob, will not give Jacob his name, and as Yahweh keeps his name hidden from Moses ("I am that I am"), so the *mal'āk Yahweh* in Judg. 13:17–18 says to Manoah: "Why askest thou thus after my name, seeing it is secret?" And after the *mal'āk Yahweh* has vanished in the flame of the altar, Manoah says to his wife (verse 22): "We shall surely die, because we have seen *God*" (italics added). In the same way Gideon (Judg. 6:22) fears to die because he has seen the *mal'āk Yahweh* "face to face." [5] The passage is in a still wider sense revealing with respect to the nature of the *mal'āk Yahweh*. It says: "And when Gideon perceived that he was the *mal'āk Yahweh*, Gideon said, Alas, O Lord Yahweh! for because I have seen the *mal'āk Yahweh* face to face. And Yahweh said unto him, Peace be unto thee; fear not: thou shalt not die."

From this and other passages mentioned above, it is clear that the *mal'āk Yahweh* is identical with Yahweh; for only in that case is Gideon's fear that he must die justified. At the same time Gideon differentiates him from Yahweh. His cry of lamentation that he has seen the *mal'āk Yahweh* is directed to Yahweh. Does this not make beautifully clear that the *mal'āk Yahweh* is identical with Yahweh and yet is not Yahweh in his all-embracing totality? He is Yahweh in a definite function, as his manifestation. He is the side of Yahweh turned toward man as a hypostasis, as it were, his function of relationship.[6] So the *mal'āk Yahweh* is Yahweh, but only one side, one aspect of his being. That is why he can appear as

5. Compare Exod. 33:20, where Yahweh says to Moses: "Thou canst not see my face: for there shall no man see me, and live."

6. This is especially clear in the aforementioned passage of Exod. 3:2 and 4. In verse 2 the *mal'āk Yahweh* is Yahweh appearing to Moses, as can be seen plainly in verse 4.

God himself, yet in another place is clearly his messenger, as his name also tells us.[7]

What is the significance of this peculiar identity of function of the *mal'āk Yahweh* and Yahweh? This question very early became the subject of theological consideration. Concerning the more ancient conceptions (Philo, Church Fathers, and others), see below (p. 71, n. 33). Gunkel, commenting on Gen. 16:7, tries to surmount the difficulty "by religious-historical considerations":

> The oldest legends speak very naturally of visions of God: Yahweh appears in person, one hears his steps, sees his form, and hears his voice. But a later time would feel it as a profanation if anything so human were reported of Yahweh himself. For this reason it relates that it was not Yahweh himself who appeared, but a subordinate divine being, his "messenger." This law of development, that certain predicates of the Godhead become offensive as religion progresses and are then bestowed upon a lower divine being, plays a great part elsewhere, too, inside and outside Israel. . . . Just because of this reflected origin the figure of Yahweh's messenger "has always remained an insubstantial phantom" (Ed. Meyer, *Israeliten*, 216).[8]

7. It has been suggested (by Vatke, de Wette, Reuss, Bertheau, Wellhausen, and others; see Hermann Schultz, *Alttestamentliche Theologie* [Göttingen, 1896], p. 476; cf. also Adolphe Lods, "L'Ange de Jahve et l'âme extérieure," *BZAW* No. 27, p. 277, who in addition mentions Procksch as a representative of this view) that the word really means "message, mission." According to its meaning, this cannot be denied; the *mal'āk Yahweh* is, so to speak, the functional expression of God, which is received by man as message. But it is scarcely possible to assume that such an abstraction is at the bottom of this concept. Its very personification speaks against it.

8. Gunkel, *Genesis* (4th ed., 1917), p. 187. Concerning this interpretation Fridolin Stier (*Gott und sein Engel im Alten Testament* [1934], p. 6, n. 16) cites also the following authors: S. M. Lagrange, "L'Ange de Jahvé," *Revue Biblique,* XII (1903), 212–25; B. Stade, *Biblische Theologie des Alten Testaments,* I, 96 ff.; R. Kittel, *HSAT*[4], I, 380, note c, on Judges 6:11; Frey, "L'Angelologie juive au temps de Jésus-Christ," *Revue des sciences philosophiques et théologiques* (1911), p. 90, n. 4; and A. Schulz, *Das Buch der Richter und das Buch Ruth* (1926), p. 40, on Judges 6:11.

This, however, would have to be verified by proving (which would be difficult) that the *mal'āk Yahweh* is in every case an interpolation. Gunkel himself admits, however, that the figure of the angel, thus created, is not so very late (Hos. 12:5; also Gen. 24:7; 48:16), so that in any case it is not permissible simply to expunge *mal'āk* from the texts as secondary in 16:7 and in related passages.[9] I can therefore see no solution to the problem in the interpolation theory.

Recently W. Baumgartner has devoted a basic study to the problem of the *mal'āk Yahweh* from a philological and literary standpoint, which in principle moves in the same direction but arrives at more differentiated results (see above, p. 58, n. 2). A comprehensive research of all the *mal'āk Yahweh* passages leads him to the conclusion that the designation *mal'āk Yahweh* does not differentiate this angel from the others. But it does differentiate the divine messenger, the messenger of Yahweh, from the ordinary messenger, as is shown by the much more frequent profane use of the term *mal'āk* in the Old Testament. *Mal'āk Yahweh,* therefore, in his view, does not designate a particular angel as distinguished from other angels, but God's messenger as distinguished from the ordinary messenger, hence simply, the angel. As a precise parallel, Baumgartner mentions the term *bēt Yahweh,* "Yahweh's house." Sometimes it is spoken of as "the house" or "my (thy, his) house," meaning the Temple as distinguished from an ordinary house. Consequently, he concludes that the translation "Angel of Yahweh (of God)," current since Jerome's time, should be discarded as incorrect.[10] I cannot, however, completely agree with Baumgartner's far-reaching conclusion that with this reinterpretation "the basis is removed for the concept of the *mal'āk Yahweh* as an angel with defined qualities."[11] In my opinion, this would be justified only if the concept by itself would explain the qualification. But the relation of the *mal'āk Yahweh* to Yahweh is also a qualifying

9. Gunkel, *loc. cit.*
10. Baumgartner, *op. cit.*, pp. 99–100.
11. *Ibid.*, p. 100.

factor; the frequent manifestations of an identity with Yahweh seem to be one of his qualities, which cannot be understood by the explanation of the concept alone. Baumgartner, like Gunkel (see above, p. 59), holds it "an error to regard this development as merely a historical process of textual changes, as has happened on occasion, which would entail simply deleting *mal'āk* wherever the word occurred." [12] Baumgartner discriminates between the antiquity of the conception, which is attested to by Hos. 12:5 [13] and by the Elohist's preference for angels,[14] and the age of the literal text. In this regard he draws attention to the fact that one must reckon with various changes, not only in the transmitted writings, but even in earlier times. So, according to him, this angel who alternates with Yahweh is certainly not earlier, but later, than the other "angels" found in ancient Israelite belief, that is numina of varying provenance who were originally independent and later subordinated to Yahweh.[15] With all these essential, philological-exegetic statements of Baumgartner, the real theological problem posed by the identity of Yahweh and his angel persists. According to Baumgartner they make "all speculative interpretations of the *mal'āk Yahweh* untenable," but I believe this does not hold for the phenomenological formulation of the problem: What does it mean that—sooner or later, whether it be in the verbal or only in the later written transmission—there ensued an equalization between Yahweh and his angel?

A further attempt to solve the *mal'āk Yahweh* problem is presented in Fridolin Stier's monograph, *Gott und sein Engel im Alten Testament.*[16] For him the identity problem is reduced, to begin with, to a question of style. The utterances of the angels in the Old Testament are messages like those of the

12. *Ibid.*, p. 101.
13. "Yea, he [Jacob] had power over the angel [*mal'āk*] and prevailed. . . ."
14. Baumgartner, *op. cit.*, p. 102.
15. *Ibid.*
16. F. Stier, *op. cit.*, p. 158.

prophets, but, in contrast to the latter, they lack the form of a message. Stier advances various reasons for this: [17]

1. A psychological factor: An unconscious slipping of the writer from the "he" style to the "I" style because of habituation to the "I" form. For example, in Deut. 29:6, in the middle of Moses' words, it says: "I am Yahweh thy God!" The writer "forgot" for a moment who was speaking and slipped unconsciously into the style of Yahweh's speech.

2. A text-historical factor: *mal'āk* may have been interpolated in front of the original "Yahweh."

3. A stylistic factor, upon which Stier places the most weight. It is a matter of the abbreviated form of the ancient oriental heraldic style. The herald speaks as if he were the sender of the message. For this Stier also gives extrabiblical examples. In the Babylonian Adapa myth [18] the messenger speaks without including the phrase: "So speaks Anu." "Since naturally interpolation does not come into question here, it is a matter of the short and pithy way the Oriental can deliver a message." [19] A condensed stylization of the herald's message is also shown in the dialogue between Ashurbanipal and a priest of Nebo. The priest says to the king: "Be not afraid, Ashurbanipal! Long life will I give thee, good breath will I ordain for thy soul." [20] From all this Stier deduces that the *mal'āk Yahweh* is a "creaturely" angel, and that the "idea of identity" is "completely excluded." Stier, however, overlooks two essential factors:

1. The identity problem cannot be reduced to a mere stylistic problem, if only because the identity is by no means exclusively expressed in spoken messages, but also in *actions* which are sometimes carried out by Yahweh and at other times by his *mal'āk* (e.g., see above, pp. 58 f.).

2. The stylistic abbreviation itself has a psychological

17. *Ibid.*, pp. 17 ff.
18. Among others Stier (*ibid.*, p. 19, n. 37) refers to A. Ungnad, *Die Religion der Babylonier und Assyrer* (1921), pp. 128 ff.
19. Stier, *op. cit.*, p. 19.
20. H. Pinckert, *Hymnen und Gebete an Nebo*, No. 2, pp. 16 ff. (*cit.* Stier, *op. cit.*, p. 20, n. 40).

background. If there were no likeness of nature implied, or at least thinkable, the language would surely have made a point of explicitly setting the two apart. The same may be said of the exchange of person assumed by Stier (see above, pp. 59 f.). Such an exchange between God-ego and God-messenger would not be possible unless the subjects had some essential connection with each other. What is psychologically important is that one is and can be taken for the other. Such an exchange is an unconscious identification.

Stier, moreover, overlooks the fact that such an "identity" exists, not only with the *mal'āk Yahweh* but even with the prophets, "the men of God," in the sense that they are the mouthpiece of Yahweh. It is as if their human individuality is extinguished at the moment of their message. The same must be assumed for the above-mentioned priest of Nebo.

Stier's objection on principle to the "theory of identity," pointing out that one ought not to apply modern concepts to old material, I find absolutely correct, as such. He says very pertinently:

> The historian tries to feel himself understandingly into the carriers of religious concepts, in order to catch what these concepts really meant to them. One may not speak in a western way before one has seen in an oriental way. The . . . quoted formulations show plainly that the Graeco-Roman impress on our thought and point of view only too easily becomes an unsolicited interpreter who tries continuously to interpose himself between us and the word of the source. Religious history is a superior art of translation, and as such is only genuine and true when it is a reproduction of the original mode.[21]

However, an essential restriction seems necessary to me. To be sure, one must let one's ideas grow out of the material, not put them into it. But in the process of grasping the material, one cannot ignore all the possibilities of understanding which have been crystallized during the subsequent cultural developments. For instance, to understand archaic thinking, as such,

21. Stier, *op. cit.*, pp. 7–8.

does not mean to think archaically oneself. Distance, not identification, is just what makes understanding possible. To be sure, on a deeper level, modern man, too, is archaic; and unless this primal human experience in ourselves is touched, a living approach to this material is not possible. However, our understanding of the material must necessarily go beyond the self-understanding of a past era, for old material contains more meaning than was conscious at the time of its origin. Can we ourselves fully grasp our own nature and the spiritual content of our time? We must immerse ourselves in the material in as unprejudiced a manner as possible, or better, with the greatest possible awareness of our own preconceptions. But we cannot avoid expressing the meanings we have grasped in the cognitive terms which our culture has created since. Concepts like "hypostasis," "manifestation," "identity," and the like can therefore be applied with full legitimacy to an Old Testament context, even though they are not Old Testament concepts themselves. Even the phenomenological approach, however, does not guarantee a final "objective truth," but it does represent an optimum. Objective truth is perhaps, in any case, an ultimate concept. The student in any discipline can only strive to come closer to it. This, in the last analysis, is probably due to the fact that the spirit has many strata and that its light breaks into many facets.

From the standpoint of religious history, Stier sees the origin of the *mal'āk Yahweh* in the Egypto-Babylonian "vizier." It would carry us too far afield to enter in detail upon Stier's discussion of this point. I shall mention only the end result of his investigation. He points to the Babylonian Nebo and the Egyptian Thoth as celestial viziers corresponding to the viziers on earth. Nebo is called *nabiu Anu* = "Anu's Herald." [22] As herald of the gods he bears the name *Pap-sukal*,

22. Jastrow, *Die Religionen Babyloniens und Assyriens*, I, 119 (*cit.* Stier, *op. cit.*, p. 135). I am indebted to Prof. W. Baumgartner of Basel for pointing out that this translation is extremely doubtful. In the first place, it does not say "herald of Anu," but "he who is called by Anu," and secondly, there is still another meaning of *nabū*, namely "shining,"

which means "highest or holy messenger." [23] The stereotype title for Thoth is "representative of Re." Therefore the vizier is an intermediate being who acts as agent between God and man. According to Stier, this also holds for the Old Testament *mal'āk*. But even this religious-historical basis for the appearance of the *mal'āk Yahweh* in the Old Testament is not sufficient to lay the "identity ghost." Nebo and Thoth are *gods* with well-defined characteristics and specific functions (see above, p. 65). Just this cannot be said of the *mal'āk Yahweh*, as will be shown later (see pp. 70 f.). The *mal'āk Yahweh* neither has a proper name of his own, nor does his function give him a distinctive character. The very concept receives its designation from Yahweh, and he has no function that Yahweh himself does not carry out in other passages. This fact alone is enough to dispel the idea of the vizier as an image for the *mal'āk Yahweh*.

A more satisfying explanation of the *mal'āk Yahweh* has been contributed by Adolphe Lods in his article "L'Ange de Jahve et l'âme extérieure." [24] He holds it to be a primitive concept, a theory that seems justified not only by the preponderance of the *mal'āk Yahweh* in the older texts but also by the numerous parallels in primitive concepts which he cites. According to these, the elements of a personality can detach themselves from it without ceasing to be connected with it. They can even constitute its life principle without the personality itself ceasing to exist. That, for example, is the case during sleep, when the soul or its double can betake itself to a distance.[25] This concept is found in the Old Testament, too;

---

which fits very well with the god of the planet Mercury, *stilbon*. (Cf. P. Jensen, "Texte z. assyr.-babylon. Religion," *Keilschriftliche Bibliothek* [1915], Vol. VI, No. 2, p. 16.)

23. Stier, *op. cit.*, p. 123.

24. Lods, *op. cit.*, pp. 265–78. According to Van der Leeuw, also, the angels belong in the category of the "exterior soul" ("Geister," *RGG* ², II, 961). Cf. also *idem, Phänomenologie der Religion* (1933), §§16 and 42, 7.

25. For this primitive concept of the "âme extérieure," Lods refers particularly to Frazer, *Golden Bough* (3d ed.), II, 441–564.

thus Ezekiel feels himself carried to Jerusalem, while his body lies in Tel-abib. In a wider sense, all the stories of mana-laden objects—like Elisha's staff, with which his servant Gehazi is to bring the son of the Shunammite woman back to life (II Kings 4:29–31), the mantle of Elijah which enables Elisha to cross the Jordan and so forth—contain the same idea. In its most primitive conception, a name is also such an "exterior soul." It contains the essence. Therefore, whoever gives away his name delivers himself up. This holds true for men as well as gods. For this reason Yahweh, too, keeps his name secret (Exod. 20:7). Hence Lods says: "Transfer this notion of 'primitive' psychology to a divine being and you have concepts which strongly resemble the concept of *mal'āk*." He cites, in particular, Exod. 23:20–21, where Yahweh says to Israel: "Behold, I send an Angel before thee, to keep thee in the way. . . . Beware of him, and obey his voice . . . for my name is in him."

In this way the *mal'āk Yahweh* comes close to the *fravashis* of the Iranian religion. "The *fravashi* of the Lord is the Lord himself; thus the epithets which pertain to Ahura are attributed, in Yasna 26, to his *fravashi*."[26]

According to Lods, the Roman conception of the genius, both divine and human, was of a similar character. It was believed that the gods visited, by means of their geniuses, the many shrines where they were invoked. Lods gives an example of this: Statius (*Silvae* III. 1. 28) makes this plea to Hercules, for whom a temple had been built: "Huc ades et genium templis nascentibus infer." And he points to the fact that this trait of the Roman genius pertains to the *mal'āk Yahweh*. Indeed, one of his main functions is to be present at the "birth" of sanctuaries (Lachai-Roi, Beersheba, and Ophra, in the story of Manoah).

I cannot agree with Lods's opinion that this concept was "utilized" in historic times to solve two theological difficul-

26. Nathan Soederblom, *Les Fravashis* (Paris, 1899), p. 56 (*cit.* Lods, *op. cit.*, p. 276).

ties, first in order to reconcile the idea of Sinai as the seat of Yahweh with his manifestations in Canaan (Exod. 23:33) and later to explain that Yahweh could be effective outside Palestine as well.[27] This assumption of Lods and the authors cited below is improbable, not only because the *mal'āk Yahweh* concept would not have been at all suitable for solving the aforementioned theological difficulties, but also because it is altogether too rationalistic to assume that such concepts were consciously created for a definite purpose. Lods speaks expressly of the "creators of the idea." [28] His evidence for the primitive characters of the concept is in itself sufficient proof that it simply was there and would preclude such a "theological problem" from coming up. Such concepts are not "made" by man any more than dreams are; they arise in him, as an expression of his inner nature. It seems that the presence of Yahweh in Sinai as well as Canaan was not the problem to the ancient Hebrews that it is to their modern interpreters, caught in their materialistic-spatial way of thinking.

An essential question, of which Lods takes no account in his clarifying article, presents itself: What does it signify *theologically* that Yahweh is represented as a person with an "exterior soul"? This is surely an extraordinarily important

27. Further advocates of this view (*cit.* Stier, *op. cit.*, p. 132) are Eduard Meyer, B. Stade, R. Smend (*Lehrbuch der Alttestamentlichen Religionsgeschichte* [2d ed., 1926]), and G. Westphal. Meyer (*Die Israeliten und ihre Nachbarstämme* [1906], p. 216) considered the *mal'āk Yahweh* as the product of a naïve theology which attempted to mediate between Yahweh's confinement to Sinai and his appearance in Canaan. According to Meyer, "he always remained an insubstantial phantom, which had significance only as a theological formula, by which it was attempted to find a way out of the contradiction between the religious postulate and the cultic practice." According to B. Stade (*op. cit.*, I, 97) the idea that Israel is led by an angel sent by Yahweh mediates between the ancient belief that Yahweh dwells on Sinai and the belief that, where Israel is, there Yahweh is also. G. Westphal (*Jahwes Wohnstätten nach Anschauung der Hebräer*, p. 31) also considered the *mal'āk Yahweh*, as a single being opposed to the popular concept of the plurality of angelic beings, to be a product of theological reflection.

28. Lods, *op. cit.*, p. 278.

fact, for it demonstrates the germ of a differentiation process in the divine personality which unfolds increasingly in the Old Testament. This process is there, quite apart from the historical inquiry as to whether the various hypostatized sides of Yahweh's being are "melted-in" ancient demons or not. The melting process could easily have taken place in such a way that the elements, as such, would no longer be visible. That they are visible is a part of the Yahweh phenomenon which cannot be grasped from the aspect of religious history alone. Precisely the *mal'āk Yahweh* seems to me to be a direct expression of the differentiation tendency inherent in the divine personality. The *mal'āk Yahweh* has no individuality of his own; in a way he exists only inasmuch as he is Yahweh's self-expression, a form of his being. His functions can therefore be most diverse: he brings revelation, protection, threat, everything which Yahweh does himself. Where a function is very distinct, the *mal'āk* is named after it, like the *mal'āk ham-mašḥīt,* who embodies the destructive function of Yahweh. Yahweh himself, at midnight, smites all the firstborn of Egypt; but he speaks of the "destroyer" who will do this (Exod. 12:23). In II Sam. 24:16 it is the *mal'āk ham-mašḥīt,* who sends a pestilence upon the land. That we have here a further differentiation of the *mal'āk Yahweh* concept, and not something different in essence,[29] is plainly shown in this passage, for in the same sentence the *mal'āk ham-mašḥīt* is immediately afterward called the *mal'āk Yahweh*. In the same way it is the *mal'āk Yahweh* who, in II Kings 19:35, slays 185,000 Assyrians in one night.[30]

It seems to me that the above-mentioned passage in II Sam. 24:16 hints at the nature of this differentiation. There it says: "And when the angel stretched out his hand upon Jerusalem to destroy it, Yahweh repented him of the evil, and said to the angel that destroyed the people [*mal'āk ham-mašḥīt bā-'ām*], It is enough: stay now thy hand. And the *mal'āk Yah-*

29. See Duhm, *op. cit.*, pp. 14 f.
30. Cf. Isa. 37:36.

weh was by the threshing place of Araunah the Jebusite." The *mal'āk Yahweh* is therefore the instrument for carrying out the divine will, the activity of God, but it is as if there arose a conflict in God, which is followed by an inner change; he repents his stern judgment. He is no longer identical with his destructive function; he opposes it by commanding the *mal'āk Yahweh* to stay his hand. Here we have already a confrontation within God himself, which takes a more pronounced form in the later Scriptures. The *mal'āk Yahweh,* as is shown most plainly here, is not a being with a will of his own. He rages automatically, until Yahweh stops him. As Yahweh detaches himself from his own function, however, it becomes discernible, at least in form, as something separate from him. It is this "split" which makes the function, as such, visible. What was said previously (see pp. 68 f.) in regard to the relation of this immanent differentiation process to the historical problem is very well illustrated here. Even if behind the *mal'āk ham-mašḥīt* there were an ancient demon of pestilence who had been assimilated into the Yahweh personality, this happened in a way that lets this demon appear as an immediate characteristic of Yahweh himself, which is shown by his identity with the *mal'āk Yahweh.* What is important in our context is that this virtually melted-down old demon becomes visible again as an aspect of Yahweh and thereby also demonstrates for us the differentiation process in the divine personality.

What has been said in regard to the *mal'āk Yahweh* can be summarized as follows.

1. He is not an autonomous being with a will of his own. He is identical with Yahweh, or with definite, delimited functions of Yahweh and sides of his nature. "God operating in a concrete place and at a definite time is called the angel of God." [31] He therefore has no personal traits of his own. He is

31. See Hitzig, *cit.* Hermann Schultz, *op. cit.,* p. 476. Stier (*op. cit.,* pp. 4–5) cites the following authors as holding the same opinion: Kautzsch, Baudissin, and Knobel. Kautzsch (*Bibl. Theologie des Alten Testaments* [1911], pp. 83 ff.) states that the *mal'āk Yahweh* is "a form

the enacted will of God which detaches itself from the Yahweh personality in the process of actualization, hence the hypostasis of God's active intervention.[32]

2. This activity of God expressed through the *mal'āk Yahweh* is not fixed in content. It covers the whole range of God's activities and partakes of his ambivalent character.

3. For the actions and words of the *mal'āk Yahweh*, as we have seen, parallels can be found in the actions and words of God himself; therefore he can be declared identical with God in his actions and words.[33]

---

of appearance of Yahweh himself, his transitory plunge into visibility, differing from him only in that he [the *mal'āk Yahweh*] cannot exhibit the full majesty of his nature." W. Baudissin (*Kyrios als Gottesname im Judentum und seine Stelle in der Religionsgeschichte* [1926–27], p. 681) sees in the angels Yahweh's form of manifestation up to the Exile. August Knobel (*Die Bücher Exodus u. Leviticus* [1880], p. 25) holds that ". . . he [the *mal'āk Yahweh*] is the divinity of Yahweh, insofar as it manifests itself, reveals itself, and has effects, so far as it enters the world of appearances and brings about something definite." Cf. also George B. Gray, *Numbers* ("International Critical Commentary" series; 1912), p. 333: "The angel of Yahweh, i.e., a temporary appearance of Yahweh in human form."

32. Also J. Rothstein (*Kommentar zum 1. Buch der Chronik*, ed. D. J. Hänel [1927], p. 380) sees the "angel of Yahweh" as the "hypostasis of a particular side of the effectiveness of the divine nature."

33. Hermann Schultz (*op. cit.*, p. 474) remarks on this: "That was so markedly beyond all doubt that the early church liked to see in this angel of God the personality of the Logos, that is, the self-revealing God himself, which here provided a prototype for the 'incarnation.' . . ." The identification of the *mal'āk Yahweh* with the Logos, the divine Word, is already found in Philo (see W. Baumgartner, *op. cit.*, p. 1, and F. Stier, *op. cit.*, p. 1). Justinus was the first to relate him to Christ (*Dialogus cum Tryphone; cit.* Stier, *op. cit.*, p. 1), and this identification became the common property of patristics. (For the pertinent passages see Stier, *op. cit.*, p. 1, n. 3.) This train of thought will later prove not to be irrelevant in our context. The angels, and especially Satan, have much to do with the mythologem of God becoming man. However, this process seems to start only with the angels as they are characterized in the concept *benē-hā-'elōhīm* and who, to a certain extent, represent a further development of this differentiation process in the divine personality, as will be shown later. But the *mal'āk Yahweh* can be seen as the nucleus of this process. It seems to me of extraordinary importance in this connection that the *human* form of the angel is stated in a number of Old Testament passages: indirectly in Judg. 6:11, "And there came the *mal'āk Yah-*

2. *The* mal'āk Yahweh *in Numbers 22:22 ff.*

In Num. 22:22 the *mal'āk Yahweh* appears in a specific negative function; he stands as an adversary in the path of the human being Balaam. However, the picture we have gained of the *mal'āk Yahweh* permits us to conclude that it is God himself who stands as an adversary in Balaam's path.

The inconsistency with which God at first gives his consent to Balaam's going to Balak, then flames into anger when he goes, may well be explained, as Mowinkel convincingly points out,[34] by the existence of two different sources for the story. Examples of such unpredictability on God's part can be found elsewhere in the Old Testament; but that here it is really a matter of two different sources is shown by God's words to Balaam in verse 32: ". . . behold, I went out to withstand thee, because thy way is perverse before me." What is happening here? The man Balaam does something according to his own will, unknowingly against the will of God; and then God obstructs his way as an adversary, as a hindrance to carrying out his own human will. The man does

---

weh, and sat under an oak . . . ," and directly in Josh. 5:13, where it speaks of a *man* who stands before Joshua with a drawn sword and later calls himself "captain of the host of Yahweh." Here, too, belong the three men who foretell to Abraham the birth of Isaac (Gen. 18:2 ff.). In Dan. 8:16, Gabriel has the appearance of a man (*geber*), and a divine *human* voice (*qōl 'ādām*) bids him explain the vision to the man Daniel (*ben 'ādām*). In Dan. 10:5 the angel again appears as a man (*'īš*). (Cf. J. Rothstein, *op. cit.*, p. 382.) In the Kabbala, one of the ten angelic categories associated with the Sefiroth is called *'īšīm*, and indeed it is the lowest, which stands closest to the human realm. In reverse, the fact that a human being can be called divine *mal'āk* throws an interesting light on the inception of the theologem of God becoming man. In Isa. 44:26 and II Chron. 36:15, 16 the prophets of Yahweh are called his *mal'ākīm*, and in Mal. 2:7 the priest is spoken of as *mal'āk*. Probably *mal'ākī* is not the personal name of the writer of the book Malachi; it rather refers to the functional term *mal'āk*. *See HSAT*[4] to the passage.)

34. "Der Ursprung der Bileamsage," *ZAW* (1929–30), pp. 233–71. Cf. also Holzinger, *Numeri* (1903), p. 104.

not see God, but his instinct, the she-ass,[35] sees him. And now God himself opens the mouth of the she-ass so that she shall warn Balaam. Every detail of this passage is so significant in our context that I shall quote it in full:

> Then Yahweh uncovered[36] the eyes of Balaam, and he saw the *mal'āk Yahweh* standing in the way, and his sword drawn in his hand: and he bowed down his head, and fell flat on his face. And the *mal'āk Yahweh* said unto him, Wherefore hast thou smitten thine ass these three times? behold, the ass saw me, and turned from me these three times: unless she had turned from me, surely now also I had slain thee, and saved her alive.

God appears here in his double aspect, as both helpful and threatening. He stands as a threat in Balaam's path, ready to slay him if he does not obey; but he helps him by opening his eyes so that he is able to obey. God puts himself in man's path in order to hinder him, but his purpose is that man comes up against him, becomes aware of his presence. Here is a mortal threat to man, but its aim is life, a life related to God. Man is literally hemmed in by God on the path of his own will; he is blinded by his own will, and it requires an act of God—the opening of his eyes—to make him perceive the will of God.

G. Westphal lays stress on the warlike character of the *mal'āk Yahweh* in this passage.[37] He sees him as warrior of the Heavenly Host, similar to the *śar-ṣebā'-Yahweh* in Josh. 5:14.

35. There are many examples in fairy tales and dreams of the riding animal as a symbol of the instincts carrying man and of the helpful animal in general as the symbol of instinct. For our context cf. Gunkel, *Das Märchen im Alten Testament* ("Religionsgeschichtliche Volksbücher," 2d ser., Nos. 23–26; 1917), p. 31.

36. Since the exact meaning of the word seems important here, I have replaced "opened" by "uncovered." *Gālā* = "to uncover," thus to take something away from the eyes which hindered vision; in our passage the vision of God. Since it is the divine will which is not perceived, one can see the blinding factor as being human self-will. This is confirmed by Num. 24:4, 16 and Ps. 119:18, where the same word is again used in the sense of opening up the vision of the divine.

37. "*ṣebā' haš-šāmaim*," *Orient. Studien II, Festschrift für Theodor Nöldeke*, p. 725.

Psychologically this would be an expression of the bellicose, "martial" Yahweh, who announces his demands like an "enemy in war," a role which is in full agreement with the profane meaning of the Satan concept, as we saw previously (see above, pp. 34 ff.). However, in our context the *symbolic* significance of the sword must also be considered.

The drawn sword seems to me to be here the symbol of discrimination evoked by the conflict between the divine and the human will. It is the symbol of knowledge. The drawn sword recalls the "flaming sword" in Gen. 3:24, where it is not carried by an angel but appears as an independent divine hypostasis. There, too, it embodies the discriminating knowledge of good and evil which separates man forever from the animal-like, innocent condition of life, for it is the Tree of Life that the sword guards. Man is cut off from the Tree of Life by his knowledge of good and evil, made manifest by the "flaming sword." [38] The *mal'āk Yahweh* appears also in II

38. Karl Budde (*Die biblische Paradiesesgeschichte* [1932], p. 84) sees *lahaṭ ha-ḥereb ham-mithappeḥet* as lightning. Correspondingly, the cherubim represent thunderclouds to him. The cherub with the sword in his hand is nothing other than thundercloud and lightning. Gunkel (*Genesis,* pp. 24 f.) goes beyond this natural-mythological conception, which, in a narrow sense, is inadequate, if only for the reason that it relates exclusively to those passages where the cherubim form Yahweh's throne (I Sam. 4:4; Ps. 18:10 [Hebrew text, 18:11]; Ezek. 10:2) and not to the more frequent passages where they have the function of guardians (in addition to Genesis 3, see Exod. 37:5–9; I Kings 6:23–27; Ezek. 28:16: "the covering cherub" *kerūb has-sōkēk*). Gunkel points to the universality of the motif of guarding the sanctuary: sphinxes at Egyptian temples and hybrid figures at the entrances to Babylonian temples. According to him the biblical cherubim are probably directly connected with these. He also sees in the flaming sword a mythical concept taken over from a foreign source. He mentions as a parallel the magic fire that surrounds Brünnhilde and—closer to the Old Testament—the brass "thunderbolt" erected by Tiglath-pileser I on the site of a destroyed city (Inscr. Tigl. Pil. I KB I, 36 f., 11. 15 ff.) which Thureau-Dangin has associated with the flaming sword (*Revue d'histoire et de littérature religieuse,* I, 146 ff.). And on Old Testament ground itself: Zech. 2:5, where Yahweh himself, as a wall of fire, watches over the future Jerusalem. Cf. also A. Jeremias (*Das Alte Testament im Lichte des Alten Orients* [1930], p. 111), who interprets *ḥereb* not as "sword" but as "magic fire," since it also means "dryness"

Sam. 14:17 in explicit connection with the knowledge of good and evil. The woman of Tekoah says, "Then thine handmaid said, The word of my lord the king shall now be comfortable: for as the *mal'āk hā-'elōhīm* (G^L and 𝔗: *mal'ak Yahweh*), so is my lord the king to discern good and bad. . . ."

In Num. 22:22, therefore, something significant happens, namely, the resistance to human will does not come from an earthly foe—as in the Solomon passages, for instance—but from God; that is, behind that which crosses the human will stands the divine will. The adversary is God himself. Here,

---

and "heat." Because of the much more frequent meaning "sword" (from the Arabic *ḥarib,* "sharp"; *ḥarbat,* "lance"; *ḥarb,* "war") this interpretation does not seem plausible to me, especially in view of the parallel of our passage in Num. 22:22 ff., where the sword also appears in conjunction with a divine being.

W. Zimmerli (*1. Mose 1–11. Die Urgeschichte* [1943], pp. 232 ff.) also points out the lightning character of the "flaming sword," yet, unlike Budde, has in mind not the natural phenomenon of lightning, but, like Gunkel, the mythologically documented protective character of fire or lightning. The closest parallel for this view is given by H. Vincent (*Revue biblique,* XXXV [1926], 481 ff., *cit.* Paul Humbert, "Etudes sur le récit du Paradis et de la chute dans la Genèse," *Mémoires de l'université de Neuchâtel* [1940], p. 40). The cherub corresponds to the Mesopotamian *Kâribu,* and the flaming sword to the lightning which forbids the way into a place and is the equivalent of the *lamassu* (*laḥmu*). The two expressions in Gen. 3:24 would therefore correspond to the "inseparable couples: *lamasu-Kâribu* posted as sentinels on the grounds of royal or divine dwellings in ancient Mesopotamia." Such a mythological classification of a motif, however, is not sufficient for a grasp of its meaning. Lightning and flame are in themselves symbols of spiritual contents. See the frequent fire symbolism for Yahweh (pillar of fire, Exod. 13:21; the above-mentioned wall of fire in Zech. 2:5; and his word as inner fire in Jer. 20:9. See also love as the flame of Yahweh [*šalhevet-Jah*] in the Song of Sol. 8:6 [the translation of the Authorized Version is not literal here]). And lightning is by its very nature the symbol of sudden enlightenment; think of the expression "flash of thought." Hence, the flaming sword symbolizes discriminating enlightenment. Looked at psychologically, too, it is the watchman of Paradise. It is, itself, that which makes a return impossible. It seems to me most interesting in this connection that, according to Tabari and others, Iblis is the guardian of the Garden of Eden! (See Leo Jung, "Fallen Angels in Jewish, Christian, and Mohammedan Literature," *Jewish Quarterly Review,* XV, XVI [Philadelphia, 1926], 34).

behind the *mal'āk Yahweh* is disclosed a dark aspect of God of a quite different kind from that seen in the *mal'āk hammašḥīt*. One can recognize here a demand of God on man which manifests itself as a threat to life and forces man to bow to this apparently destructive will.

A very similar story from Central Asia referred to by Gunkel[39] is interesting in this context. It tells of Täktäbäi Märgän, whose horse recoils abruptly when it sees the devil Ker Jupta. The youth, perceiving nothing, twice asks the horse what it has seen; finally it answers, "Look *above,* look *below*" (italics added).

Behind the close interrelation of the human and the divine will in the story of Balaam there lies, it seems to me, a profound meaning of universal human significance. In experiencing an opposition to his own will, man really knows that he has a will. By this he is lifted out of the animal into the human realm, i.e., into the experience of individual existence. The human will becomes conscious through its collision with the divine will, by coming up against the adversary. Thus, behind the deadly threat of the divine opposition there is also hidden a positive, purposeful aspect; the adversary, as such, is at the same time the creator of individual consciousness. But why must the human will be broken at the moment when man first becomes aware of it, or be apprehended only to be broken? The answer is not yet apparent from our passage. It only gives a hint that a problem of life is at stake, perhaps *the* problem of man's life; for Balaam's disobedience would have led to his death. That for God, too, it is not merely a question of prestige whether or not man obeys him, but a fateful decision, can only be dimly sensed at this point. It will become clear as we proceed, however. In my opinion this whole context of ideas provides the premise for the further development of the adversary as a mythological figure in the story where he first appears as "Satan," and which tells us the most about him: the framing story of the Book of Job.

39. *Das Märchen im Alten Testament,* pp. 31 f. (*cit.* Leo Frobenius, *Im Zeitalter des Sonnengottes* [1904], pp. 133 f.).

Satan as One of the *benē hā-'elōhīm*

1. *The Age of the Concept*

OUR THESIS that the figure of Satan represents the result of a process of development within the divine personality itself would seem to be controverted by the one passage which has made the Old Testament Satan generally known: the framing story of the Book of Job, the so-called popular Book of Job.

In general, the figure of Satan in the Book of Job is viewed as an ancient demon of popular belief, as, for example, by Hans Duhm.[1] This view is shared alike by those who assume a great antiquity for the framing story and those who, though placing it at a later time, still consider that the figure of Satan stems from an old folk tradition. The fact already discussed, that the figure of Satan has as yet no proper name in the Book of Job but acquires it only in a later work, the Chronicles, speaks strongly against the assumption of the great age of this figure. Moreover, as we have seen, the significance attached to it is very different from that of the true cacodemons in the Old Testament. These play a peripheral role. They hop about here and there like will-o'-the wisps. Though there is evidence that offerings were still made to them in the time of the prophets, this only proves that their place was outside the Yahweh religion (see above, pp. 35 ff.). But the Satan of the

1. "Die bösen Geister im Alten Testament" (diss., Tübingen, 1904), p. 17: "The most ancient form of this being must be recognized in the Satan of the popular book of Job." For this Hans Duhm cites Bernhard Duhm, *Das Buch Hiob,* pp. vii f.

Book of Job stands face to face with God in a dialectical discussion. It has been repeatedly pointed out [2] that he is subordinate to Yahweh, but this statement does not give the full picture as long as the *power* possessed by this demon, who is subordinate in rank to Yahweh, is completely overlooked. After all, he is able to incite Yahweh to turn against Job, to cause him to make a momentous decision. Yahweh lets himself become involved in a serious discussion with this demon and be influenced by him. It is true that Yahweh continues to have faith in Job; but, looked at psychologically, is there not, in the very acceptance of the wager, a concession to Satan's doubt? If there had been no secret uncertainty to rouse his interest in the outcome of this truly immoral wager at the expense of his servant Job, he would most probably have refused to engage in it.

The difficulties which this passage gives contemporary researchers may be illustrated by one example. Bernhard Duhm writes about it in his *Hiob-Kommentar:*

> If it is really too offensive to assume that the author of Job ascribed Job's misfortune to a weakness of Yahweh, who lent credence to the first-come suspicion, one should probably conceive of the writer's train of thought as follows: Yahweh has indeed the personal conviction that his

2. For example, by Hans Duhm, *op. cit.*, pp. 19–20: "The relationship of Satan to Yahweh, of the *ben hā-'elōhīm* to the highest God, may be compared to the relationship between vassal and great king. Yahweh alone has the power in his hands; without his sanction Satan is powerless." He assumes that "an older concept giving more free play to Satan must have had to adapt itself gradually to the basically monotheistic character of the Yahweh religion, which was becoming more powerful. As long as Yahweh was not yet such an unlimited, absolute monarch, Satan could still carry on his dangerous game to his own liking. . . . But more and more he lost his independence. The Yahweh religion subordinated him, like the rest of the demons, to the highest God. From then on he had to restrict himself to playing the role of denouncer before the highest judge, and, on occasion, of penal official, in order to satisfy his appetites at least in this way." Similarly Gunkel writes (*Das Märchen im Alten Testament* [1917], p. 84): "This figure, which may be of Babylonian origin, may have originally carried on its wild play on its own account before the Yahweh religion put it into the service of this god."

> servant Job is righteous from the heart and not out of self-interest, but Satan is right in claiming that an objective, decisive proof, valid also for a third party, is so far lacking. Satan (and the public opinion of the low-minded people he represents) has a right to demand a test before he, too, is convinced; and God's justice and impartiality compel him, against his inclination, to accede to the inquiry and submit his favorite to torture. Job is made unhappy because God is just; just, that is, also toward the opinion of subordinate beings whom he does not brutally suppress by his superior knowledge.[3]

This explanation does not seem to me in any way to "save" the situation. Such a concession to Satan and "the public opinion of the low-minded people he represents" would suggest the idea of weakness rather than justice, quite apart from the fact that Duhm's argumentation is nowhere supported by the text. If God's superior justice would induce him to give way, how is his reproach to Satan, for moving him to destroy Job without cause, to be explained? Can one really still see in the fact that Yahweh gives Satan permission to destroy Job an expression of the sovereignty of God? It is true that, according to his rank, Satan is a servant of Yahweh, with no independent power to act on his own; but seen psychologically, he is really the stronger. He is the servant who can persuade his master. Yahweh's reproach becomes quite evident in chapter 2:3: ". . . thou movedst me against him, to destroy him without cause." He accuses Satan of having seduced him to an act which he really repents—only to allow himself to be "incited" by Satan on a further occasion toward even more far-reaching decisions! It is scarcely possible to regard this as a demonstration of Yahweh's omnipotence. An old Talmud teacher seems to me to have had a finer sense for the atmosphere of the story than those who belittle the significance of Satan in this text. He remarks, in regard to chapter 2:3 ("Thou movedst me against him, to destroy him without cause"): "If it were not in the Bible, one would not be

3. B. Duhm, *op. cit.*, p. 9.

allowed to say it"; for God is represented "like a man who lets himself be seduced by another." [4] Gunkel must also have sensed the atmosphere given in this situation. He writes:

> This wager sounds as if it had not originally been agreed to by a servant and a master high above him, but much more as if concluded between two equals. This impression is also supported by the fact that in this story Yahweh and Satan speak together without regard for the immeasurable distance between them.[5]

He explains this as possibly being due to the fact that the story may be derived from an old fairy tale. "Such words are more easily understandable if they are exchanged between a man's guardian deity and his evil demon." But that for Gunkel, too, this does not answer the problem of the theological significance of these words is shown by a further explanation, which, however, is unsatisfactory because it starts from the very assumption it intends to prove: "The Job-poet may have then inserted them [these words] because in this way he could depict the insolence of Satan, which allowed him such irreverent language against the Most High." But why did he have to depict this "insolence"? What is significant is that there is room in the Yahweh concept for this impudent Satan who is *permitted* to address Yahweh in such fashion; in other words, that this idea of Satan is theologically tolerable.

Hence, compared to the ancient demons in the Old Testament, Satan has an important and new significance. Quite apart from the development of his name and the fact that the concept has its origin in the profane realm, it can surely be stated that Satan cannot possibly be a figure of long standing in the Yahweh religion.[6] He is a theological novelty, only to

4. Jochanan Bab. Bathra 16a, *cit.* Isaak Wiernikowski, "Das Buch Hiob nach der Auffassung des Talmud und Midrasch" (diss., Breslau, 1902), p. 36.

5. Gunkel, *op. cit.*, p. 85.

6. Roskoff (*Geschichte des Teufels* [1869], I, 186) has already said of the Book of Job, as was mentioned earlier (see above, p. 7), that it shows "an important turning point in the Hebrew view. . . . The ancient Hebrew belief ascribes all power only to Yahweh." He sees in

be explained by the development of the concept of God already shown. Had there been no change in the concept of God, such a story could never have come into being. It would simply have been incompatible with the older image of Yahweh. In Amos 3:6 it says: ". . . shall there be evil in a city and Yahweh hath not done it?" And even in Deutero-Isaiah (Isa. 45:5–7) we find the particularly forceful formulation: "I am Yahweh, and there is none else. . . . I form the light, and create darkness: I make peace, and create evil: I Yahweh do all these things." Of this the story of Job itself is another proof. In the consciousness of the pious Job in the framing story, there is as yet no room for the concept of Satan. Job himself ascribes to Yahweh the misfortunes that assail him, a most important point in our context, which will be dealt with further.

Yet, though Satan cannot be proved an ancient demon in the Old Testament, we would not have dealt adequately with the question of the age of this concept if we did not, by a comparison with other sources, investigate the possibility of a foreign influence upon its origin. We have yet to examine the question whether there is any evidence in the phenomenology of the Old Testament Satan for his kinship or even identity with a deity outside the Old Testament.

An early attempt to derive the Old Testament Satan from the Egyptian Seth—with no sequel in modern literature so far as I could discover [7]—is found in an article by Diestel: "Set-Typhon, Asahel und Satan: Ein Beitrag zur Religionsgeschichte des Orients." [8] From the rich material, which Diestel has drawn chiefly from Plutarch, I shall mention only the main features of what seems to him to prove his thesis that Satan is Seth, as adopted by the Old Testament.

---

this an indication that this book cannot possibly be held to be one of the oldest in Hebrew literature.

7. Cf., especially, Gerhard Seippel, *Der Typhonmythus* (1939). (See below, p. 84, n. 12, and p. 86.)

8. Diestel, "Set-Typhon, Asahel und Satan: Ein Beitrag zur Religionsgeschichte des Orients," *Zeitschrift für die historische Theologie*, XXX (1860), No. 2.

The opposition of Osiris and Seth, the beneficent and the destructive, searing sun, had also very early accquired a political connotation. Osiris is the guardian deity of Egypt; but the opposite of Egypt is the world outside its borders, so Seth appears in his capital as the god of foreign countries. He is described as colorless, pale, yellowish.[9] According to Diestel, pale, yellowish figures on Egyptian monuments always depict northern foreigners.[10] Diestel believes that the Egyptian concept of Seth evoked the idea of Satan as it must have appeared in the first form of the Job legend. A close geographical connection making such a transition possible seems to him to be provided by the circumstance that the Land of Uz in the Book of Job is most probably located in the south; while the Egyptians, for their part, very early carried on mining operations in the Sinai peninsula, the border area between Judea and the Nile land, which necessarily entailed extensive settlements. Moreover, at a later period, Seth's abode, as well as his worship, was transferred to these northeasterly boundaries. Here Diestel cites the mythological tales of Seth being chained in the Sirbonian Sea[11] and his flight to Syria and Palestine.[12] It seems to him equally easy to prove the similarity between the two figures of Seth and Satan, but at this point certain doubts arise. First of all, he restricts the similarity to Satan's activities in the Book of Job in bringing the evils about. He names all five of them: the raid of the Sabeans, the fire of God, the raid of the Chaldeans, the wind from the wilderness, and the boils. Without noticing that the first four blows against Job do not proceed directly from Satan, and although he himself says that, according to the analysis of

9. Plutarch *De Iside et Osiride* 33.

10. *Op. cit.*, pp. 200 ff.

11. Herodotus III. 5; *cit.* Diestel, *op. cit.*, p. 172.

12. Plutarch *De Iside* 19. 5; *cit.* Diestel, *op. cit.*, p. 176. Cf. also Theodor Hopfner, *Plutarch über Isis und Osiris*, II, 143 ff. Hopfner, however, like G. Seippel (see above, n. 7) does not draw from the Semitic relations of Seth the same conclusions as Diestel regarding the Old Testament Satan.

Num. 16:35; I Kings 18:18; and II Kings 1:10 and 12, the "fire of God" can mean only lightning, Diestel, citing Ewald, interprets it as originally "a sudden sultriness and heat falling from the air." [13] "It is a deadly, searing, fiery heat, which can very quickly do away with men and beasts. Just this is the most prominent characteristic of Set." [14] Any doubt, however, about this "fire of *God*" coming from Yahweh, especially in view of the parallels mentioned by Diestel himself, is scarcely possible. He further lays stress on the fact that Job's cattle were taken by robber hordes from the northeast and southeast, that is, by foreigners. And Seth is the god of the hostile outland, also precisely of the south and the north. For Seth as a parallel to Satan, who is expressly characterized as the bringer of boils, Diestel can find support only in a very general statement from Plutarch that Seth is the bringer of all inhibition, disturbance, and destruction.

Diestel's conclusion, "It thus proves that almost all the essential evils inflicted by Satan also constitute the activity of Set," [15] is therefore not convincing. But the failure of his attempt shows most clearly when he construes an identity between the names of Seth and Satan, "since the first may be connected with *šūt*, *šīt*." [16] How this could become *śāṭān*, Diestel explains as follows: ". . . in order to designate this religious concept, in a Semitic country a strictly Semitic word was adopted, which at least offered a similarity of sound, together with fitting characteristics." [17] Nothing could be less likely, however, than just this, that *śāṭān* should, because of a similarity of sound, be an arbitrarily selected covering name for Seth.

According to Diestel, this adoption occurred very early. In that case it would at least have been the result of an uncon-

13. Diestel, *op. cit.*, p. 210.
14. *Ibid.*
15. *Ibid.*, p. 211.
16. *Ibid.*
17. *Ibid.*

scious process. But this contradicts everything we have been so far able to establish concerning the Satan concept and its development, above all its originally profane usage.

Yet perhaps it is not for nothing that the figure of Seth is brought into our context, if one does not, like Diestel, pin down its influence on the Yahweh religion to Satan, but poses the question in a more general way. Then the parallel to Yahweh *himself* immediately becomes striking. Among other animals associated with Seth, Diestel speaks of the crocodile and the hippopotamus.[18] Is it not perhaps here that in Yahwism itself the trace of Seth can be found? For as Leviathan and Behemoth—whose names, among others, have been thought to be Egyptian (see above, p. 43)—they are attributes of Yahweh in Job 38. Egyptian influence is perceptible in several passages of the Book of Job, and for this reason it has even been assumed that its author was an Egyptian.[19] In these two mythological figures—Leviathan and Behemoth—appears the wild nature-side of Yahweh. In addition, it is interesting that Behemoth and Leviathan are also akin to the mythical sea monsters and that one of these, Rahab, appears as a direct personification of Egypt (Isa. 30:7; 51:9; Pss. 87:4; 89:10), i.e., as the turbulent sea. But in Egypt also Seth was held equivalent to the sea. He is the sea "in which the Nile (Osiris) dissolves as he flows out and disappears altogether." [20]

Gerhard Seippel refers to another interesting trait shared by Seth and Behemoth (not Rahab, as he assumes) in Job 40:18: "Seth's bones are the iron which yields the material for weapons and is symbolically equivalent to Seth's fighting power." [21] It is said of the hippopotamus which Yahweh has made (Job 40:18 ff.): "His bones are as strong pieces of brass; his bones are like bars of iron." Satan, however, is not himself

18. *Ibid.*, pp. 169–70; Plutarch *De Iside* 32.
19. See Gustav Hölscher, *Das Buch Hiob* (1937), pp. 7–8. Also Paul Humbert, *Recherches sur les sources égyptiennes de la littérature sapientale d'Israël* (1929), pp. 75 ff.
20. Plutarch *De Iside* 32; *cit.* Diestel, *op. cit.*, pp. 169–70.
21. Seippel, *op. cit.*, p. 136.

the dark nature force symbolized in all these images; he is rather a spiritual differentiating principle in God which causes God to become aware of his own nature side. This will become still clearer with the further exegesis of the Book of Job. Yahweh appears in yet other passages as the vanquisher of Rahab, of Leviathan and Behemoth, also in the Book of Job itself,[22] but here what has been conquered has become an aspect of his own nature. He overcomes his own nature side by knowing about it. Here lies an eminent psychological truth, which is experienced as a mythologem in the God personality. On another plane, such a self-conquest of Yahweh also occurs in Zech. 3:1 ff., as will be shown later (see below, p. 144).

The decisive factor of the originally profane usage of the Satan concept also makes a *Babylonian* origin of the Satan figure extremely improbable, at least for the first stage of assimilation, i.e., for the unconscious adoption of Babylonian Canaanite conceptions after the settlement in Canaan (see above, pp. 103 f.). It is still to be considered, however, whether Satan may nevertheless be an ancient Babylonian concept which became assimilated (though only after the Exile; that is, in the second stage of Babylonian influence) as an adequate expression of the Old Testament development of the concept of God. A seemingly close parallel to the Book of Job thrusts itself upon our attention, the "Poem of the Righteous Sufferer," the so-called "Babylonian Job."

A king is smitten with sickness.[23] He describes his torments

22. Job 26:12. Cf. also Pss. 74:14; 104:26; Isa. 51:9.

23. Morris Jastrow assumes that it is a king ("A Babylonian Parallel to the Book of Job," *Journal of Biblical Literature,* XXV [1906], 135–91; see also his *Die Religion Babyloniens und Assyriens* [Giessen, 1912], II, 106 ff., and particularly p. 121), on the basis of other examples of "royal lamentations." See also S. Landersdorfer ("Eine babylonische Quelle für das Buch Job?" *Bibl. Studien,* XVI [1911], 55–59), who also follows up the reasons for this assumption in detail; and likewise Robert W. Rogers (*Cuneiform Parallels to the Old Testament* [2d ed., Abingdon Press, 1926], p. 164, n. 1). St. Langdon ("Babylonian Wisdom," in *Babyloniaca: Etudes de philologie assyro-babylonienne,* ed. Ch. Virolleaud [1906–37], VII, 131–95: "The Babylonian Poem of the

in a great song of lamentation to the gods which, after he has been freed from his suffering, ends in a hymn of praise to the "Lord of Wisdom." There is no doubt that the "pursuer" in Tablet II refers to a demon of disease:

> All day the pursuer followed me,
> At night he granted me no respite whatever,
> Through wrenching my joints were torn apart,
> My limbs were shattered and rendered helpless.[24]

The first question that arises—whether with the Book of Job and especially with the figure of Satan we have to do with a direct literary borrowing—is answered in the negative by both Jastrow [25] and Landersdorfer.[26] The latter maintains

---

Righteous Sufferer") does not share this general opinion of scholars, but holds that the suffering hero of the poem was "simply an influential resident of the ancient city of Nippur" (p. 135). For the most recent English translation of this text, see "I Will Praise the Lord of Wisdom," trans. R. Pfeiffer, *Near Eastern Texts Relating to the Old Testament*, ed. James B. Pritchard (2d ed., Princeton University Press, 1955).

24. Jastrow, "A Babylonian Parallel to the Book of Job," p. 171. Pfeiffer translates similarly in *Near Eastern Texts . . .*, p. 435, vss. 37–40:

> "All day a pursuer pursues me.
> At night he does not let me draw my breath for a moment.
> Through straining my sinews have been loosened,
> My limbs are wrecked, hit aside."

Cf. also Landersdorfer, *op. cit.*, p. 24, vss. 66 ff.:

> "The whole day the persecutor pursues me,
> In the night he does not let me breathe a moment (in peace),
> My joints are dissolved by maiming. . . ."

Similarly Ebeling, in Gressmann, *Altorientalische Texte zum Alten Testament*, p. 276, vs. 104:

> "The whole day the persecutor pursues me,
> In the night he does not let me breathe a moment (in peace),
> By tugging back and forth my sinews are torn apart,
> My limbs are burst apart, and thrown aside."

25. *Die Religion Babyloniens und Assyriens*, II, 133: "The presentation offered here of this section of Babylonian-Assyrian literature leads to the conclusion that a direct influence of Babylonian-Assyrian songs of lamentation and repentance prayers upon biblical creations cannot be spoken of." Compare, though, his earlier, less assertive view, espe-

that, "probably in one case as in the other, we have a more or less free retelling of a folk legend, such as one finds by the dozen in the literature of all culture groups." His final conclusion is:

> There is no basis for assuming any literary dependence, direct or indirect, of the biblical Job upon the Babylonian "Poem of the Righteous Sufferer," since the similarities shown by the two texts can be explained just as well, and less arbitrarily, as stemming from the natural development of the subject of the story, especially considering the great number of important disparities and the lack of positive proof of any dependence.[27]

The Indian parallel of King Harishchandra (see below, pp. 93 f.) and that of the Egyptian "Conversation of a World-Weary Man with his Soul (Ba),"[28] both of which likewise raise the problem of the righteous sufferer, confirm Landersdorfer's view that we have here a *typical* motif found in many religions.

---

cially concerning the "Poem of the Righteous Sufferer" in his earlier essay ("A Babylonian Parallel to the Book of Job," pp. 190 f.): "Literary influences, however, may be potent without necessarily pointing to direct borrowing, . . . Literary influence, reinforced by the possession in common of an indefinite amount of folklore, legendary lore, and ancient traditions, suggests itself as a satisfactory solution of the problem involved in a comparison of the story of Tabi-utul-Bel, and the treatment of the theme of human suffering there found, with the strikingly parallel story of Job."

26. Landersdorfer, *op. cit.*, p. 126. Cf. Samuel Terrien, "The Book of Job: Introduction and Exegesis," *The Interpreter's Bible* (Abingdon Press, 1954), III, 881: "Since the Akkadian poem was well known before the Babylonian exile (n. 42: Several copies of it were made during the seventh century B.C., and the existence of a philological commentary explaining the archaisms of its language points to its relatively wide circulation. The exact date of its composition is uncertain, but it is considerably older than Job.), it is possible that the biblical poet was acquainted with it, but no trace of literary dependence can be demonstrated."

27. Landersdorfer, *op. cit.*, p. 138.

28. In A. Erman and F. Krebs, *Aus dem Papyrus der königlichen Museen zu Berlin* (1899), p. 54; cf. "A Dispute over Suicide," trans. John A. Wilson, *Near Eastern Texts Relating to the Old Testament*, ed. James B. Pritchard (2d ed., Princeton University Press, 1955), pp. 405–7.

However, neither the universality of the basic theme of both poems nor the improbability of a direct dependence of the Book of Job upon the Babylonian poem suffices to resolve the problem of possible Babylonian influence. Might not the sickness demon—to whom the sufferings of the king are ascribed in the Babylonian song of lamentation—represent an ancient concept adopted during the Exile and finding expression in post-Exilic biblical writings, in our case in the Book of Job? This possibility has led Hölscher, as before him Hans Duhm and others, to the conclusion that the Satan in Job "is a demonic figure who is thought of as the originator of all evil, especially of sickness." [29] Yet it should already be clear from what we have observed thus far that the Satan in Job is by no means exclusively, or even primarily, a sickness demon. It seems to me, moreover, that consideration of the inner content would lead us to exclude not only a literary dependence of the Job Satan on the Babylonian lamentation, but also any *tale quale* adoption of the "persecutor" concept. The essential differences in theological structure and atmosphere between the two poetic writings can become apparent only when seen against the background of a complete picture of the character of Satan in the Book of Job (see below, pp. 133 f.). Yet it seems to me very probable that the Babylonian sickness demon, as the primal image of *one aspect* of the Job Satan, namely, as the bringer of sickness, forms a part of this picture. In this respect he will concern us again later (see below, pp. 133 ff.).

Although our investigations have shown that Satan as a complex phenomenon cannot be derived from any traceable extrabiblical ancient demon, yet there is a quite different aspect to the question of the age of the concept which must be dealt with. Just as the motif of the Righteous Sufferer is found in different religions (shown by Landersdorfer's research into the "Babylonian Job"), so also the motif of the divine wager in myths and fairy tales is unmistakably wide-

29. Hölscher, *op. cit.*, pp. 2–3.

spread. As was mentioned earlier (see above, p. 82), Gunkel [30] points out the fairy-tale character of this story.[31] August Wünsche [32] has followed up this particular motif. According to him it stems from a twofold root: On the one hand from the early Christian dogma of atonement, according to which Satan's defeat is represented as his being outwitted by the Redeemer [33]—in that Christ, by his sacrifice, cheated Satan of his rights toward men, won by the first man's sin—and on the other hand from old Germanic religious beliefs. Here it was originally the giants who were outwitted by the gods. After the spread of Christianity the giants were replaced by the devil, who, in many Germanic tales, is stupid, as are they. As is made plain by the many stories of various provenance about the cheated devil which Wünsche cites, the motif of the wager as a test of strength between divine and demonic potencies, is universal; psychologically speaking, it is archetypal. Wünsche holds it to be a "migrating motif" (*Wanderstoff*), a theory controverted by the very examples he gives. For the Christian wager motif could not possibly have given rise to the Germanic versions, nor the latter to the former. Wünsche's work itself demonstrates the inadequacy of the "migration theory." Wünsche expressly rejects "Bastian's theory of elementary ideas which presupposes an independent origin for the legendary tales out of the universality of human nature," although without giving his reasons. But Bastian's idea has long since been confirmed by C. G. Jung's concept of the archetypes and substantiated by him with an abundance of mythological and dream material. The archetypes are the expressions of primal human experiences, which can occur everywhere on earth. The motif of the divine

30. *Op. cit.*, p. 85.

31. Cf. also Oskar Dähnhardt, *Natursagen* (1907), I, 177 ff. and 347 ff.; Johannes Bolte and Georg Polívka, *Anmerkungen zu den Kinder- und Hausmärchen der Brüder Grimm* (1918) (to No. 189: "Der Bauer und der Teufel"), III, 355 ff.

32. A. Wünsche, *Der Sagenkreis vom geprellten Teufel* (1905).

33. The various versions in the New Testament Apocrypha and by a number of Church Fathers; see *ibid.*, pp. 3–9.

wager is also such an archetype; but what would it express? It seems to correspond to a phase in the development of human consciousness in which the opposites have separated and become apparent but in which there is as yet no stability. It still is *uncertain* who is the stronger. The good must still *prove* itself stronger than the powerful evil, cleverness stronger than stupidity, and consciousness struggling out of unconsciousness must maintain itself against the darkness of the unconscious. This contest situation can be accounted the common basis for the Germanic, Old Testament, and Indian wager motifs.[34] Such archetypal motifs, however, are molded by cultural-historical conditions into forms which can differ widely. For example, in the Germanic legends and fairy tales Wünsche cites, where the devil is cheated of his wages, he is usually stupid and is defeated by cleverness. Wünsche says:

> A kinship between the mythological sagas of giants and the Christian legends about the devil is vouched for, above all, by the stupidity which is characteristic of both. Just as the giants, with all their strength and force, are clumsy, stupid creatures who are outwitted and cheated by the clever little dwarfs as well as by the intelligent gods, so in most legends which show the devil entering into a wager, he shows himself to be a stupid creature who does not grasp the full range of the wager and so draws the short end.[35]

However, there is no such contrast between intelligence and stupidity as far as God and Satan in the Book of Job are concerned. As will be shown, Satan is an eminent spiritual potency and a "divine being." Furthermore, in its Christian version, seen from the examples cited by Wünsche, this motif is greatly refined and deepened. The essentially different character of the Satan wager in Job from that of the Germanic-Christian legends of the devil is involuntarily demonstrated by Wünsche when he lists it among the latter as a "small

34. For India, too, has its wager tales. See above, pp. 92 f.
35. Wünsche, *op. cit.*, p. 82.

deviation." [36] Of the "delightful humor" which Wünsche claims for the legend cycle of the cheated devil,[37] nothing is to be sensed in either the early Christians forms of the motif of the devil's wager or in the Book of Job. Gustav Hölscher, who in his *Hiob-Kommentar* also stresses the humor of this motif, probably proceeded less from his own immediate feeling experience when reading the Job story than, like Wünsche, from the impression made on him by the Germanic legends of the devil, without noticing that here a very different wind was blowing. God's wager in Job is a desperately serious matter, as I have already tried to show (see above, pp. 80 ff.).

There are two parallel stories which come closest in content to the wager episode in the Book of Job and, in addition, have in common with it the motif of the piety test.

1. A Swahili legend relates that the archangels Gabriel and Michael disagreed as to whether there was still compassion to be found among men. Michael doubted it. They descended to Earth, Gabriel as a very sick man and Michael as a physician. Michael tells the sympathizing citizens that the sick man can be cured only by a human sacrifice. A boy shows himself ready for it, and now Michael's doubts are overcome.[38]

2. The Indian tale of the trials and wonderful patience of King Harishchandra relates the following: [39]

36. *Ibid.*, pp. 82–83.

37. *Ibid.*, Preface. Wünsche does, however, mention that it is above all the German legends which bring out this humor.

38. See Paul Volz, "Hiob und Weisheit," *Schriften des Alten Testaments,* (1921), p. 9. The legend is also given in detail by Carl Meinhof, *Die Dichtung der Afrikaner* (1911), pp. 85 ff.

39. In the Markândeya-Purâna. See Paul Volz, *op. cit.*, pp. 8–9. The story is told in more detail by Konstantin Schlottmann (*Das Buch Hiob* [1851]), to whom Volz refers; see also A. Jeremias, *Das Alte Testament im Lichte des alten Orients* (1930), pp. 328–29, and others. (For complete references see Adolphe Lods, "Recherches récentes sur le livre de Job," *Revue d'histoire et de philosophie religieuses* [1934], pp. 501–33.) Schlottmann (*op. cit.*, p. 18) thinks, however, that an influence of Christian missionaries is not out of the question, since the scene in Heaven, which recalls Job, is not found in the older versions, not even in the Purânas, but only in the later dramas.

> Once the gods and the holy penitents were assembled in Indra's Heaven. An argument arose between them, whether there existed on earth a completely virtuous prince. Vasishtha claimed that his student Harishchandra was such a one, but Siva, who was present in the guise of Vismamitra, answered angrily that the virtue of this man would not stand a severe test. The gods deliver Harishchandra up to him and Vismamitra goes to work. He does the king a service for which he asks an enormous sum of money; and Harishchandra promises to pay it to him. But because, again and again, he is unable to pay it, he and his wife sink into the deepest misery. Both finally become slaves, and the king has to carry out the most despised task existing, that of burying the dead. But he takes it all upon himself for the sake of his promise, for "there is no higher duty for a man than the duty of keeping his word." Likewise, supported by his noble wife, he sustains the test until the end; he gets back wife, child, and kingdom and along with all his people is raised to heaven by the gods. So in the end, as the poem says, the greatest suffering is turned to the greatest joy.

The emergence of an archetypal motif and the form it takes are thus, as these parallels show, not unaffected by history. They are the expression of an inner process of development, whether in the dreams of an individual or in the myths and theological conceptions of a people. In our case the mythologem of God's wager is an expression of the development in the divine personality of Yahweh, as will become clearer later on. Were this not so, how could we explain the fact that the Yahweh religion did not adopt a great deal more from the vast store of legends and myths? Why, for instance, in this land of the cult of fruitfulness par excellence, where the idea of the *hieros gamos* was so alive and present, was Yahweh never given a companion goddess? [40] The reason is that such an acquisition would never

40. Elephantine cannot very well be taken as an example, since it represents a relatively late, independent, special development of a separated branch of the people's totality, though as such it is indeed most remarkable.

have been tolerated because it would have represented a regression to a pre-Yahwistic concept of God. It is most important to discriminate between the first stage of development, the merging of a multiplicity of good and evil demons in the divine personality of Yahweh, and a later stage of development, in which the unity of this divine personality re-enfolded into a multiplicity under the influence of the polytheistic environment. But this influence was only possible on the basis of the inherent development of the divine personality. In the new multiplicity, however, the formerly established unity is not lost, as is shown, for example, by the fact that the angels are subordinate to God. It is this second process to which, as was previously pointed out, the Satan figure essentially belongs. Even if it were a matter of an ancient demon figure alive at this stage, it would in any case have become something altogether new and different as soon as it became part of the concept of God. Hence the problem is shifted from that of the age of the Satan concept, as such, to that of the time of its appearance in relation to Yahweh. To put the problem in this form is justified since, as was said before, there is no evidence whatever in the Old Testament itself for the mythological concept of Satan outside his relation to Yahweh.

2. *The Age of the Text*

THE GREAT MAJORITY of scholars regard the framing story of the Book of Job as ancient, because of its folktale character, but a few have begun to doubt it. Thus Hölscher finds it hardly possible to place the framing story far back, in a very ancient time, merely on the basis of the differences between it and the poem. An equally late composition of the framing story is shown by its dependence on the Priestcodex (Job 42:17: "So Job died being old and full of days") and by an Aramaism like *qibbēl* (Job 2:10).[41]

41. Hölscher, *op. cit.*, p. 5. He cites K. Kautzsch (*Das sogenannte Volksbuch von Hiob Cap. 1; 2; 42:7–17* [1900]), who (pp. 24 ff. and 40 ff.) points out a still later verbal usage on the grounds of which he

The same view is held by Ernst Sellin, not for the whole framing story, but in regard to the Satan passages,[42] which he takes to be interpolations into the folktale by the author of the poem.[43] He draws especial attention to four points which support his assumption:

1. From a purely textual standpoint the two Satan passages can be conceived of as interpolations (without this counting as proof) because they can be omitted from the context without leaving a gap. But of foremost significance to Sellin is the fact that 1:13 connects directly with the last verse before the Satan passage; that is, with 1:5. There it is told how Job offered sacrifices, also having in mind the sins which his children might commit. Then, if the Satan passage is omitted, it goes on consistently: "And there was a day when his sons and his daughters were eating and drinking wine. . . ."

2. If the Satan story belonged to the original legend, the Epilogue would have to refer back in some way to the wager with Satan. Sellin says on this point: "In the folk legend it would have been an absolutely essential element that God

---

considers erroneous the assumption that the poet of Job had before him a "folk book." He believes that the poem and the framing story stem from the same hand. The latter may have been known to the poet as an older *oral* tradition (p. 87). Kautzsch takes the Satan passages to be one of the strongest pieces of evidence against the theory of the pre-Exilic origin of the Prologue (p. 58). The post-Exilic origin of the Prologue, in which Satan appears, is also assumed by Erik Stave (*Ueber den Einfluss des Parsismus auf das Judentum* [Haarlem, 1898], p. 249 and n. 1), citing E. König, *Einleitung in das Alte Testament* (1893), pp. 410 ff., §84, 2a. Cf. also W. F. Albright in his review of Hölscher's "Hiob-Kommentar," in the *Journal of Biblical Literature*, LVII (1938), 227 f.; and J. Hempel, *Die althebräische Literatur* (1930), p. 176.

42. E. Sellin, *Das Problem des Hiobbuches* (1919).

43. Cf. also Norbert Peters, "Das Buch Job," *Exegetisches Handbuch zum Alten Testament* (1928), p. 49*. Joh. Lindblom, also, considers it certain that the Satan episode was inserted into the primitive story but believes that the author of the Job poem found it already worked into the ancient tale (in its Israelite traditional form; cf., below, p. 122, n. 85). He bases this on the fact that Satan is not mentioned in the dialogue—failing, as I believe, to recognize the *inner* connection of the Satan episode of the framing story with the essential problem presented in its dialogue. (On this, see below, p. 124.)

should have scolded him for his unjustified defamation, while the poet was concerned only with a later enlightenment of Job." [44]

3. The reason for interpolating the Satan passages is a theological one. The author needed them as an indispensable element, now usually not appreciated, for building up his theme.[45]

4. Satan comes onto the scene exclusively in post-Exilic times, and his appearance among the angels matches exactly that in Zech. 3:1 ff. The conception of Satan as the bringer of all evil to mankind does not agree with ancient Israelite thought, according to which everything whatever, good and bad alike, was the act of God (Amos 3:6; II Sam. 24:1),[46] so it can scarcely be looked for in an ancient folk legend.[47]

We can follow Sellin's conception in detail only as we come to analyze the text. It appears to me to do the most justice to the facts and to receive further confirmation by the name factor, which Sellin does not mention. In his theological exposition of the inner connection between the framing story and the poem, however, he arrives at conclusions with which I cannot entirely agree. According to Sellin, Satan has the function of unburdening God of evil,[48] so to speak, which in my opinion is seeing the problem too simply (cf. below, pp. 118 ff.). But Sellin's principal statement seems to me of essential significance here: that there exists a close connection between the Satan figure in the framing story and the theological problem of the poem. Where, from my point of view, this connection is to be found will be discussed later.

The foregoing may be summarized as follows: Most scholars have separated the question of the age of the text from that of the Satan concept and have been correct in doing so. However, there is the further necessity to discriminate be-

44. Sellin, *op. cit.*, p. 23.
45. *Ibid.*
46. Most clearly formulated in Isa. 45:7. Cf. above, p. 83.
47. Sellin, *op. cit.*, p. 23.
48. *Ibid.*, p. 36.

tween an older and a later stratum of the Satan concept. The parallel motifs found in other myths and fairy tales have shown us the primeval character of the basic concept (see above, pp. 90 ff.). Sellin pays no attention to this factor. On the other hand, those who emphasize the age of the concept ignore the fact that it is ancient only in its primal form, as archetype, and not in the very definite shape it has in the Book of Job. They completely overlook the theological novelty that this basic archetypal motif represents within the Yahweh religion, while Sellin's mistake is that he does not recognize the archetypal character of the motif, treating it as an invention of the author of the Book of Job. Each of these one-sided points of view neglects something essential; the supporters of the "ancient demon," however, commit the more serious omission. It seems to me necessary to combine these two points of view: The story is a variation of an old basic motif of popular belief. In the form given here it is not, however, a theologically unimportant relic of a popular belief that has been overcome by the Yahweh religion; it is rather a mirror of an essential stage of development in that religion.

We must therefore ask: In what way is this archetypal concept of demons "built into" the Yahweh religion?

The very fact that we are not dealing here with just some indiscriminate figure, detached from Yahweh, that comes to meet him by chance, but with one belonging to a specific Old Testament category of divine beings, demonstrates the complete recasting and further development of this archetypal figure. For the Old Testament Satan is one of the *benē hā-'elōhīm*. He is an *angel*. To understand his significance, we must begin by inquiring into the nature of the *benē hā-'elōhīm*.

3. *Occurrence and Nature of the* benē hā-'elōhīm *in the Old Testament*

THE PROBLEM of the *benē hā-'elōhīm* is, if possible, still more complex than that of the *mal'āk Yahweh*. It would burst the frame of this work to follow it into all its ramifications. Only those points of reference will be studied which appear to be relevant to Satan as one of the *benē hā-'elōhīm* in the Book of Job. Let us turn first to the concept as such.

Gunkel, in his commentary on Genesis,[49] refers to the possibility that behind the concept there may be an older polytheistic verbal usage which was applied in the literal sense to sons of gods, that is, to beings begotten by gods. But he gives preference to the other assumption derived from Hebrew usage, according to which the *benē hā-'elōhīm* should be conceived of as "beings belonging to the category of *'elōhīm*." B. Duhm terms the *ben hā-'elōhīm* "a single being (*Einzelwesen*) in the divine sphere." [50] In connection with the term for a species, in Hebrew an individual belonging to this species is designated *ben*. Thus, *'ādām* means man in the generic sense, hence mankind; *ben 'ādām* refers to a single creature of the species man, that is, the individual man, not the son of man. Nevertheless this verbal usage remains an interesting problem in itself. It is as if behind it there were a primal image of the relation of the species to the individual, and that is the relation of father to son. The species *begets* the individual, so to speak. There is really behind it something like a substantial Platonic idea, only personified in a graphic image. This personified idea of the species is manifested in the individual being, as is the father in the son. Seen from this possibly underlying archetypal background, the translation with "son" becomes meaningful again. The son of man is then the idea "man" realized in the individual, and the son of God is the realized manifestation of God.[51] In our context both

49. Gunkel, *Genesis* (4th ed., 1917), p. 17.

50. B. Duhm, *op. cit.*, p. 6 (see n. 1, above).

51. From this point of view, there is meaning and weight to the idea of the Paulicians or Bogomiles, a neo-Manichaean sect, according to which it was not Christ but Satan who was the firstborn son of God. Euthymius Zigadenus reports as follows: "Dicunt, daemonem, qui a Servatore appellatus est Satanas, Filius esse ipsum quoque Dei Patris et vocari Satanaël, et Filio Verbo natu majorem esse, praestantioremque, utpote primogenitum . . ." (*Panoplia* 23. See Migne, *Patrologia Graeca*, CXXX, col. 1290; quoted in the Latin translation by Du Plessis from

meanings—*ben* as part of the species and as son—open up interesting theological aspects and do not exclude each other; but the concept "son" is more graphic and so more "alive." That this usage of the word is not confined to the theologically prominent concepts of "God" and "man," which would make the situation less conclusive, is shown, for example, by the concept *ben bāqār:* "a single member of the herd," or *benē han-nebī'īm,* which does not mean "sons of prophets" but "those belonging to a group of prophets." [52] It is therefore the designation of a single creature of the species in the image of the son.

So the *benē hā-'elōhīm,* the sons of God, are divine beings, "single beings of the divine sphere" (B. Duhm), parts of the God-substance. Hence, like the *mal'ākīm,* they may be understood as a mythological expression of aspects of the divine nature. However, while the *mal'āk* appears time after time as God himself in carrying out the divine intention, the *benē hā-'elōhīm* are always around God. They are, in a way, the substance of the inner divine totality divided into its single elements. This is expressed by the fact that they surround God as a "heavenly assembly."

At the same time, however, there is a hint of an essential difference between the *benē hā-'elōhīm* and the *mal'āk Yahweh.* As the term *benē hā-'elōhīm* shows in itself, this process of divine partition is not associated with the individual name of the God Yahweh but with the divine name of *'elōhīm,* whose originally pluralistic form can still be recognized. There is nowhere any mention of *benē Yahweh.* This suggests the assumption that in the multiplicity of the *benē*

Christoph Ulrich Hahn, *Geschichte der Ketzer im Mittelalter,* I, 48, n. 1). The idea had already found an early formulation among the Ebionites: "Duos ut iam dixi, a deo constitutos assereunt, Christum et diabolum" (Epiphanius *Panarium* 30, published and translated by Franciscus Oehler [1859], I, 267).

52. I Kings 20:35; II Kings 2:3, 5, 7, 15; 4:1, 38; 5:22; 6:1; 9:1. Gesenius-Buhl, *Hebr. und aram. Handwörterbuch über das Alte Testament* (1915), *s.v.,* translates with "Angehörige der Prophetengenossenschaft"; the Zürich Bible says: "Prophetenjünger."

hā-'elōhīm is expressed the original plurality of the concept of God, i.e., that behind them are hidden ancient pre-Yahwistic gods, a plurality of *'elōhīm.* This assumption is beautifully confirmed by two parallel passages. The closest connection is given in Ps. 89:7, where the sons of God are called *benē 'ēlīm,* i.e., divine beings or sons of gods; and *'ēlīm,* in contrast to *'elōhīm,* can be understood only as plural. Moreover, *'ēl* is an ancient North Semitic name for a god.[53] This leads to the further parallel of Psalm 82, where they are simply called "gods": *'ēlōhīm.* God, *'elōhīm,* stands in the congregation of gods, *ba-'adat 'ēl,* and "judgeth among the gods," *'elōhīm.* In the same psalm, verse 6, they are also called *benē 'elyōn,* a name of God which probably designates an ancient deity of Jerusalem (see Genesis 14, the god of Melchizedek). That we are dealing here with what were originally pre-Yahwistic deities, in whose designation, in contrast to the *mal'ākīm,* we can still see not only the differentiation process but also the merging process which preceded it, can be confirmed by still further parallels.

The *benē hā-'elōhīm* constitute, in their homogeneous multiplicity, the "host of heaven": *ṣebā' haš-šāmaim.* The fact that these two concepts can even be equated is shown in I Kings 22:19, where, in the vision of Micaiah ben Imlah, the heavenly court assembly is called *ṣebā' haš-šāmaim* in the same situation where Job 1:6 and 2:1 speaks of the *benē hā-'elōhīm.* We can see that probably behind this heavenly host were originally ancient astral deities, since various passages speak of the sun, moon, and stars as the *ṣebā' haš-šāmaim,* to whose worship men should not let themselves be seduced.[54]

53. For more on this subject see Julian Morgenstern, "The Mythological Background of Psalm 82," *Hebrew Union College Annual,* XIV (Cincinnati, 1939), 39, n. 22.

54. Deut. 4:19; 17:3; II Kings 17:16; 21:3, 5; 23:4; Zeph. 1:5; Jer. 8:2; 19:13; Job 31:26–28. In connection with the divine name *Yahweh ṣebā'ōt,* the *ṣebā' haš-šāmaim* has led to a discussion which, so far as I can see, has not yet reached an end nor found a satisfactory solution. G. Westphal pursues the problem in a thorough study ("*ṣebā' haš-*

šāmaim," *Oriental. Studien II, Festschrift für Theodor Nöldeke* [1906], pp. 719–28). He reaches the conclusion that it originally had to do with a heavenly warrior host that joins Yahweh in battle, corresponding more or less to the "wild host" (*wilden Heer*) of German fairy tales, to which Gunkel calls attention. It is from this heavenly host that Yahweh has the name *Yahweh ṣebā'ōt*. Westphal bases his theory chiefly on Josh. 5:14, where the *śar ṣebā' Yahweh* is spoken of, who, as the "chief of the host of Yahweh," approaches Joshua as the leader of the earthly army. The term *ṣebā' Yahweh,* then, would have been applied to earthly armies only later. Westphal points out that those passages where the earthly host is obviously meant are of a later date (Exod. 7:4; 12:17, 41 = P; and Judg. 16:13). Many particulars support Westphal's thesis, as, for example, the *maḥanē 'elōhīm*, the place of God's host in Gen. 32:3. Also his understanding of the chariot of fire and the horses of Elisha (II Kings 2:11) in this sense has much to recommend it. Nevertheless his solution of the problem will not do. A weak point in his line of argument lies, above all, in his failure to find any satisfactory explanation for the other, nonwarlike functions of the *ṣebā' haš-šāmaim:* "This expression, doubtless originating during the period of the conquests, was then adapted to the contemporaneous ideas about the duties and activities of the 'heavenly host'; so, in I Kings 22:19 ff. the *ṣebā' haš-šāmaim* has an advisory activity, later it is given the task of continuous praise of Yahweh, as in Pss. 48:2; 103:20 ff. Then, when under Manassah the Babylonian-Assyrian star worship penetrated into Judah and Jerusalem, the old expression, which had lost most of its content, was found suitable for the designation of this new cult object." The last statement in particular seems to me completely improbable. Westphal does not sufficiently consider the close connection of the *ṣebā' haš-šāmaim* concept with that of the *benē hā-'elōhīm*. Neither does he do justice to the greatly predominating usage of *ṣebā' haš-šāmaim* for the stars. His reference to the heavenly host as originating in meteorological powers, i.e., the stars as auxiliary troops of the thunder-god Yahweh (for which he chiefly cites Judg. 5:20, where the stars, from their courses in heaven, fight against Sisera) is far from sufficient. The many passages which speak of star worship show plainly that this had to do with the concept of stars as *gods*. A textual observation by Schrader (*Der ursprüngliche Sinn des Gottesnamens Jahwe Zebaoth.* [n. d.]) weighs heavily against Westphal's thesis; namely, that the plural *ṣebā'ōt* is only used for earthly armies, never for the heavenly host. Schrader therefore holds the divine name *Yahweh ṣebā'ōt* to be synonymous with "the God of the armies of Israel," in I Sam. 17:45, to which it forms an expressive parallel. Eichrodt also refers to this (*Theologie des Alten Testaments* [1906], I, 94). Another confirmation of the fact that *Yahweh ṣebā'ōt* was originally the designation of a *war* god is seen by Eichrodt in the circumstance that this byname of Yahweh's is always used in close connection with the Ark (I Sam. 4:3–5 ff.; II Sam. 6:2), which for a long time served as a war palladium. But Eichrodt comes up against the difficulty that the war-god concept does not explain the verbal usage of the

Historically, as has already been mentioned in another connection, the process probably has to be understood as an absorption of a multiplicity of ancient deities, i.e., all the hypostatized forces of nature, into the divine figure of Yahweh. After this original merging process, these deities come to constitute the elements of a new structure and find their place in it. The historical imprint stemming from an ancient context receives a new coloring in the new system, or else is entirely recast. The example of the *benē hā-'elōhīm* nicely illustrates the interesting fact that ideas tabooed and fought against as idolatry throughout the whole Old Testament become "legalized" when at certain moments in the Yahwistic development they can be assimilated unconsciously, so to speak, and without friction, to serve as *a fitting image* for a phase in the Yahwistic process of development. So, on the one hand, the worship of stars is condemned as idolatry (see above, p. 101 and n. 54) and, on the other, the image of the heavenly host is reabsorbed very early (Josh. 5:14; I Kings 22:22). We can therefore justifiably assume that the concept of the heavenly court and the divine council meeting could only have been adopted because it was needed as a fitting mythologem for the beginning of an inner process of differentiation in the godhead. It arises, as it were, of itself, out of the Babylonian-Canaanite ideas unconsciously absorbed after the settlement in Canaan.

The Babylonian Exile is a second phase of assimilation, which again must be thought of as an unconscious occurrence

---

prophets. He sees no other possibility than to assume that *ṣebā'ōt* does not refer to specific armies, but to hosts, masses, multitudes in general, the sum total of all earthly and heavenly beings, as it was also understood in LXX: *κύριος τῶν δυνάμεων*. Perhaps we have here the actual solution of the problem, especially in view of Genesis 2:1, where it speaks of "the heavens and the earth and . . . all the host of them." L. Koehler (*Theologie des Alten Testaments* [1936], p. 33) decides for the assumption: *Yahweh ṣebā'ōt* means "Lord of the Stars," which, according to him, implies a negation of the pagan idea that the stars are gods. But this assumption again does not take into account that the heavenly host never appears in the plural. So the problem appears to be still unsolved.

in view of the conscious attitude of resistance to the enemy conquerors and their culture during just that period. That an unconscious infiltration nevertheless took place is best shown by Ezekiel, who was the pillar of the exiles' inner battle for survival and whose vision, insofar as it is a spontaneous manifestation of the unconscious, is suffused with Babylonian concepts. Such are probably the chariot of God, the vision of vocation, the recording angel, and so forth, unless one follows the presentation of Lorenz Dürr,[55] which is, in my opinion, too rationalistic. Dürr, in effect ignoring the *vision* character of these contents, takes them rather as an expression of conscious theological deliberation, i.e., the transference of Babylonian cult traits to Yahweh. This seems to me wide of the mark. The infiltration of mythological contents is also shown, perhaps especially clearly, in the visions of Zechariah in the Priest Codex account of creation, where behind the Tehom can still be recognized the Tiamat hidden within it, and where Yahweh forming the cosmos out of chaos takes the place of Marduk overcoming Tiamat and dividing her into heaven and earth. To be sure, here, too, the reshaping into the specifically Yahwistic becomes particularly clear; but the Babylonian mythologems are, as *images*, indispensable statements about the nature of the Old Testament God. Zimmern [56] also distinguishes two phases of Babylonian influence on Yahwism when he derives the Old Testament concept of the angelic host from the Babylonian one of the "Igigi (and Anunnaki) assembled around the highest god, partly as an advisory assembly and partly as a host of war." He adds: "At a *later* time, beginning with the Exile, the Israelite concept of angels was again strongly influenced by Babylonian mythology" (Zimmern's italics).

In this way the *benē hā-'elōhīm*, originally stemming from the pluralistic concept of God, *'elōhīm*, became, after the smelting process, aspects of the nature of Yahweh. Hence the

55. *Die Stellung des Propheten Ezechiel in der israelitisch-jüdischen Apokalyptik* (1923).

56. Schrader, *KAT*, p. 457.

meaning of their name should not be overvalued at this level. They are no longer a plurality of separate nature powers but are the power of nature in Yahweh himself, his aspect of creative but also destructive nature, so to speak. Even more plainly than in the "Host of Heaven," whose mythological character is not further described, this is shown by other examples. The seraphim, for instance, who in Isaiah's theophany (chapter 6) surround the throne of God, corresponding to the *benē hā-'elōhīm* in the passages cited above, can still be recognized as definitely mythological animal deities.[57] They literally belong to the image of the appearance of God, that is, to his totality. That at the same time they stand as servants about the enthroned king shows that the divine personality has grown beyond the solely natural. He has become the holy God. However, this holiness in him is not torn out of nature but is rooted in it. And nature bows down to this holiness, as seen in the "Holy! Holy! Holy!" of the seraphim in Isaiah's vision. Historically, it is the overcoming of the old nature divinities by the spiritual God Yahweh; but it also indicates Yahweh's development from a nature god to the holy God. This phenomenological wholeness is incomparably expressed in the Isaiah vision.

Less closely connected than in Isaiah 6, and without the completeness of a genuine vision capable of adequately expressing the whole of a living paradoxical unity, the same phenomenon appears in the *neḥuštān,* which probably represents an ancient serpent deity. The difference between it and the Isaiah vision is very revealing, however. The legend in II Kings 18:4—that it is Moses' brazen serpent—is intended to

57. Their origin has so far not been established with any certainty. One is generally inclined to assume that it has to do with snakelike fabulous animals (see Hans Duhm, *op. cit.,* p. 4; Baudissin, "Die Symbolik der Schlange," *Studien zur semitischen Religionsgeschichte,* I, 282; Johannes Nikel, *Die Lehre des Alten Testaments über die Cherubim und Seraphim* [1890], p. 88), as is suggested by the name *śārāf,* which perhaps refers to the burning bite of the animal. A convincing analogy, however, is given by the *neḥāšīm haś-śerāfīm,* the seraphs of the wilderness (Num. 21:4–6 and Isa. 30:6, where the flying serpent is spoken of (*śārāf me-'ōfēf*). On the name, cf. also above, p. 44.

strengthen its connection with Yahweh. Yahweh sends the serpents and makes Moses erect the *neḥaš neḥōšet*. That a later, religiously more differentiated, time recognized that this connecting of the *neḥuštān* with Moses was merely a thin veil thrown over what was originally a serpent cult is shown by Hezekiah's fight against it. He has the *neḥuštān* broken to pieces, in the same "cleansing operation" in which he does away with the holy high places, breaks the images, and knocks down the Asherim.[58] The link between the old serpent divinity and Yahweh was not sufficiently close and organic. As a *separated* nature cult it could not be tolerated by the more developed Yahweh religion. At that period the separation of Yahweh's nature side and its independent worship really signified a regression to an earlier stage.

Corresponding to the seraphim in the Isaiah vision, the cherubim in Ezekiel's vision, grouped around God's throne, i.e., carrying it, constitute his living unity of nature and spirit. They are also the guardians of Paradise, of the divine realm of nature from which man was expelled. And in Ps. 18:10 a cherub is the animal ridden by Yahweh: "And he rode upon a cherub, and did fly: yea, he did fly upon the wings of the wind." In I Sam. 4:4 and II Sam. 6:2 Yahweh also appears throned upon the cherubim.

So the cherubim and seraphim are a particularly clear example of old nature deities which have become aspects of Yahweh. By their parallel function they confirm our conception of the "heavenly host" surrounding Yahweh and of the *benē hā-'elōhīm,* who, by their function, are a close parallel to it and who are our special concern here.

Hence, to be constantly surrounding Yahweh is the first characteristic which differentiates the concept of the *benē hā-'elōhīm* from that of the *mal'āk*. The *mal'āk* appears almost exclusively as a single figure. He is mainly, as his name already shows, the emissary sent by God on particular occasions. It should be noted that this holds also for almost all the

58. Sacred poles, set up near the altar; see Koehler-Baumgartner, *Lexikon in veteris testamenti libros* (Leiden, 1958), *s.v.*

passages where the plural is used. In Gen. 28:12, too, the *mal'ākīm* are not described as surrounding God; they are also his messengers or his heralds; they climb up and down the ladder, thereby, so to speak, announcing the appearance of God. Their character of messenger is very clear in Ps. 78:49: Yahweh casts upon Egypt his "anger, wrath, and indignation, and trouble, by sending evil angels" (*mišlaḥat mal'ākē rā'īm*).[59] *Mišlaḥat,* the mission, gives further support to the messenger character already implicit in the term *mal'āk.* This becomes explicitly clear also in Ps. 91:11: "For he will give his angels (*mal'ākīm*) charge over thee. . . ."[60]

There are, however, two passages which suggest an earlier association or partial equating of the two categories of angel:

1. The *śar ṣebā' Yahweh* in Josh. 5:14. According to the concept, he might belong to the *benē hā-'elōhīm,* but he reminds us of the *mal'āk Yahweh* by his particular function, by the sword in his hand of Numbers 22, but, above all, by his stated identity with Yahweh which is characteristic of the *mal'āk Yahweh,* for he speaks almost the same words to Joshua that Yahweh addresses to Moses in Exod. 3:5: "put off thy shoes from off thy feet; for the place whereon thou standest is holy ground."

2. Gen. 32:2, where the *mal'ākīm* are spoken of as *maḥānē 'elōhīm.*[61]

In all other passages, however, such clearly differing characteristics of the two concepts of angels can be recognized that the two passages given above can only be evidence for the beginnings of a fusion which, as has already been mentioned, was clearly completed in the later writings.

However, the *benē hā-'elōhīm* also appear as messengers. So in the vision of Micaiah ben Imlah it is the "spirit" that is commissioned to entice Ahab; and in the Book of Job,

59. This passage is, by the way, one of the finest proofs that the angels are "aspects of God's being" and at the same time his "messengers."

60. Cf. also Pss. 103:20 and 104:4.

61. Cf. on these two passages, above, pp. 101 f., n. 54.

Satan also functions as messenger. It is precisely these examples, however, that bring out an essential difference, which leads back to our main trail, that of Satan as one of the *benē hā-'elōhīm.* For even if one of the *benē hā-'elōhīm* or the *ṣebā' haš-šāmaim* undertakes to deliver a message, he is not, like the *mal'āk Yahweh,* a blind instrument carrying out Yahweh's will—the arm that does Yahweh's deed, so to speak, or the mouth that speaks his word. He is more like a person, more autonomous; he seems to have a will of his own. Yahweh has a relation to him; he talks with him. This is not the case with the *mal'āk,* except in Zechariah, where the *mal'āk Yahweh* as *angelus interpres* exchanges question and answer with God. But this is only, as it were, a form of the relation of God to man. Here, too, the *mal'āk Yahweh* is a messenger; it is not a matter of a truly dialectic conversation between him and God. This is a subtle difference, but one of far-reaching significance, as we shall see later. The difference becomes plain if we look more closely at Micaiah's vision (I Kings 22:19 ff.):

> I saw Yahweh sitting on his throne, and all the host of heaven standing by him on his right hand and on his left. And Yahweh said, Who shall persuade [literally "entice," as in RSV] Ahab, that he may go up and fall at Ramoth-Gilead? And one said on this manner, and another said on that manner. And there came forth a spirit, and stood before Yahweh, and said, I will persuade him. And Yahweh said unto him, Wherewith? And he said, I will go forth, and I will be a lying spirit in the mouth of all his prophets. And he said, Thou shalt persuade him, and prevail also: go forth and do so.

What is interesting about this conversation in the heavenly court is that there are obvious divergencies of intention. Yahweh wants to entice Ahab. But he does not simply send a *mal'āk* to accomplish this; he seems, as it were, dependent on one of the heavenly host's offering to undertake it. The task does not appear to be very desirable, for "one said on this manner, and another said on that manner"; that is, most of them talked themselves out of it.[62] One, the "spirit" (*hā-ruaḥ;* the very *nomen appelativum* is sufficient to show that he is a being who stands out in the multiplicity of the others [63]) declares himself ready. That God's question as to who shall entice Ahab is not just a matter of democratic formality, but of a real need for the "spirit," is shown by the fact that Yahweh does not simply give a detailed command; the volunteering messenger must also contribute the idea of how to go about it.

This passage seems to me to offer an extraordinarily interesting presentation of an inner conflict in the deity, which is most enlightening in regard to the development of the God

62. This, it seems to me, is what the sentence implies and not, for instance, that positive suggestions are brought forth from the side of the *benē hā-'elōhīm;* for there can be only one answer to God's definite question, an equally definite declaration of readiness, which then actually follows, in a surely not accidental contrast to the indefinite remarks of the others, on the part of the "spirit."

63. J. Benzinger's conception (*Die Bücher der Könige* [1899], p. 124): "By this spirit, who is among Yahweh's servants, only that spirit can be meant who in general inspires and drives the prophets," seems to me too abstract. Kittel expresses himself similarly ("Die Bücher der Könige," *Nowack-Handkommentar* [1900], p. 175): "The divine spirit of prophecy, with which the prophets are filled, becomes an independent person, similar, say, to the divine quality of wisdom which becomes an independent hypostasis in Proverbs 8. As the judgment of God's anger is personified in the angel that destroyed the people (*mašḥīt*), so here the divine spiritual effect is personified in the 'spirit.' " Kittel, after all, does not overlook the personal character and the independence of this spirit. The distinct individuality of the latter is justly given the main weight by Julian Morgenstern (*op. cit.*, p. 40, n. 25): "*Haruah*, literally, 'the wind'; actually in a number of biblical passages the winds are designated specifically Yahweh's 'messengers' or 'angels' (cf. Pss. 104: 3–4; 148: 8; also Ps. 18:11 [= II Sam. 22:11]; Job 30:22). However, since it is clear beyond all question that here *haruah* has a certain individuality and personality and is commissioned by Yahweh to perform, not a general and routine service, such as winds might normally be expected to perform, but a very specific and realistic task, it undoubtedly brings out the full implication of the passage to render *haruah* here 'the,' or better 'a certain' spirit." Kaupel's argument: "If a person were meant, one could not say that the lying spirit was put in his mouth" (*Die Dämonen des Alten Testaments* [1930], p. 68), with its unfortunate mixing-together of the real and the mythological plane, can surely claim no more than a curiosity value.

concept in the Old Testament. If we take this discussion at the heavenly court as representing a divine soliloquy (a conclusion justified by the parallel in Gen. 1:26: "Let us make man in our image," where it is now generally assumed that God is speaking to the angels around him [64]), it is clear that in this matter of Ahab's enticement God is not at one with himself. "And one said on this manner, and another on that manner." So one side of Yahweh does not want to go along. There is a conflict.[65]

However, the "spirit" *wants to* and also knows how. He appears like a personification of an evil thought of God. The dark, demonic side of God begins to emerge from the ambivalent mixture with his light side and to show itself as a distinctly dark "spirit." But so far there is only a conflict in the "heavenly host," that is, between the different sides of God's being, and not between himself as consciousness and any single tendency in him. This further stage is reached only in the conception of Satan in the Book of Job. There we witness a contest between Yahweh and Satan, and it is a pointed dialectical encounter, a real speech by God and counterspeech by the adversary. In contrast to the "spirit," who is distinguished only by his ad hoc function as "lying spirit," Satan is given a sharper outline by his more definite name and also by his function. But phenomenologically the "spirit" in

64. This passage at the same time provides a valuable support for our understanding of the essential sameness of God and his angels, i.e., the identity of part and whole. A beautiful piece of evidence from Midrash Gn Rabba VII on Gen. 11:7 is cited by Leo Jung ("Fallen Angels in Jewish, Christian and Mahommedan Literature: A Study in Comparative Folk-Lore," *Jewish Quarterly Review*, 1924–25, p. 481): R. Ami says: "God took counsel with his own heart."

65. This, for example, raises Yahweh above Zeus, who carries out a similar undertaking quite untouched by any moral consideration, by sending Agamemnon a lying dream which, when it is followed, leads the Greeks to destruction (*Iliad* ii. 5 ff.). But it also raises Yahweh above himself, insofar as he at other times carries out acts of annihilation exactly like Zeus. (For the many examples see Volz, *Das Dämonische in Jahwe* [1924].) At the same time, the difference in motive must be seen: in Zeus a so-to-speak divine, unpredictable whim; in Yahweh the plan of salvation for Israel.

Micaiah ben Imlah's vision may be regarded as a direct antecedent of the Satan figure.[66]

Here belongs also the evil spirit from God who troubles Saul, after the (good) "spirit of God" as charisma has departed from him. Two diametrically opposed effects of God replace each other, thereby revealing their common root, the ambivalent divine personality. That this alternation of the two aspects of God depends on the behavior of men gives this passage special theological significance. And, as will become apparent, it also connects this story with the story of Job (see below, pp. 118 ff.).

In the fragmentary account in Gen. 6:1–4, the *benē hā-'elōhīm*—though they do not appear as a distinct will, separate from God himself—perform on their own an act which is not commanded by God but is even contrary to his will. They saw "the daughters of men that they were fair; and they took them wives of all which they chose." [67] Hence

66. Cf. also Julian Morgenstern (*op. cit.*, p. 32): ". . . he [i.e., Satan] represents here [i.e., Job 1:6–12 and 2:1–7a] a natural development from the figure of *haruaḥ* in I Kings 22:19–23." A connection in the development between the two figures, in which he includes the serpent in Genesis 3, is seen also by G. Kittel (*Geschichte des Volkes Israel* [1927], III, 141). Karl Marti ("Zwei Studien zu Sacharja," *Theologische Studien und Kritiken* [1892], p. 230) disagrees with this opinion. His line of argument, that the "spirit" in I Kings 22 does not stand like Satan in opposition to Yahweh, proceeds from the incorrect premise (on this, see below, p. 152) that Satan appears for the first time in Zechariah, and therefore he cannot weaken the point of view expressed above. No more tenable is Kaupel's negative position (*op. cit.*, p. 96, n. 1): "But if here were really the first step toward a belief in Satan, one would expect that in II Chron. 17:22 ff. *haś-śāṭān* would have been inserted in place of *hā-rūaḥ*." It is another failure to understand the connection of development, though in reverse direction, when Friedrich Schwally ("Zur Quellenkritik der historischen Bücher," *ZAW*, XII [1892], 159 f.), basing himself on B. Stade (*Geschichte des Volkes Israel* [1906], I, 531, n. 1), expresses the improbable conjecture that in I Kings 22, instead of *rūaḥ*, "there had originally been *śāṭān* or a real angel name, Michael or the like."

67. On the basis of this passage Kaupel (*op. cit.*, p. 136) denies the angel character of the *benē hā-'elōhīm*. The term is supposed to mean "the pious ones." This opinion is already found in a Zadokite tradition which was disseminated especially by Syrian authors since Ephrem;

they represent an *independent impulse.*[68] They follow a desire, a drive aiming toward the human kind. Behind God's back, as it were, they unite with human beings. From the psychological point of view this expresses a still unconscious urge in God toward men, which is also suggested by the *multiplicity* of the angels as aspects of God. It is not a conscious inclining of God toward men, as in the later theologem of God becoming man, but an unconscious urge. Therefore the union does not result, as it does later, in a God-man, but in monsters. Yet, psychologically, this passage may be claimed as a pre-form of the later theologem.

It has often been pointed out as illogical that God did not, as was to be expected, punish the angels, but instead punished mankind by shortening its span of life.[69] But the inner context

---

according to it, the *benē hā-'elōhīm* in the Book of Enoch were not angels, but sons of Seth, who because of their piety were called the "sons of God" (see Adolphe Lods, "La Chute des anges, origine et portée de cette speculation," *Congrès d'Histoire du Christianisme* [1928], pp. 32–33). But the age of this assumption is no evidence against its unscientific nature. It is a Midrash which elaborates the story of Gen. 6:1–4, and not a scientific thesis.

As such, however, it is advanced also by J. W. Rothstein ("Die Bedeutung von Gen. 6:1–4 in der gegenwärtigen Genesis," in *Festschrift für Karl Budde, BZAW* No. 27 [1920], pp. 150 ff.), but it is not convincing. Apart from other improbabilities he argues for, which it would lead us too far to go into here, Rothstein above all misses the typically mythological character of the fragments in question, as well as the inner relation of the *benē hā-'elōhīm* in this text to other statements about this category of angels. Kaupel, too, finally can find no other way out than to assume, in reference to the Job passage where the *benē hā-'elōhīm* are beyond any doubt angels, a lack of uniformity in the use of words (*op. cit.*, p. 133).

68. Cf. also C. H. Toy ("Evil Spirits in the Bible," *Journal of Biblical Literature,* IX [1890], 22): ". . . but the 'sons of Elohim' act without reference to the supreme God; . . ." Also Toy sees in their independence an essential difference between them and the *mal'āk:* "While the term *mal'āk* describes those superhuman intelligences who act as agents or representatives of God in his control of affairs, the 'sons of God' are mentioned in other connections, not so much as ministers, but rather as members of the divine court, attendants on God yet in a sort *independent*" (italics added).

69. Cf. the view of Julian Morgenstern, that the passage had originally told of the punishment of the angels. See pp. 114 f.

seems to me to make this completely consistent: One side of God wants to unite with man, the other does not want this at all, since this would make man equal to God. Hence: "My spirit shall not always strive with man. . . ." (Gen. 6:3). This, too, illustrates beautifully how the *benē hā-'elōhīm* are spirit of God's spirit. It is the same problem as in Gen. 3:1, where the one side of God—namely the dark one, the serpent—wants to seduce man so that he will become like God and know good and evil; but the other side, for that very reason, expels man from Paradise. The serpent was very early,[70] out of a correct intuition, identified with Satan, although the text gives no direct basis for it. But indirect hints unquestionably are found in the Satan passages in the Old Testament. Such an indirect connection is the one just observed between Genesis 3 and Gen. 6:1–4, which leads us to the further one between Genesis 3 and the Satan of the Book of Job, who is also one of the *benē hā-'elōhīm.* Satan, like the serpent in Paradise and the *benē hā-'elōhīm* in Gen. 6:1 ff., is set on *changing the relation of men to God.* In the Old Testament, God himself, through his dark side, works on man as "the power that always wills the bad, and always creates the good." For although the sin of Adam and Eve is the sin par excellence in the Paradise story, God depends on this very sin of man, of knowing good and evil, to carry out his plan of salvation. In the Job folktale, Satan is not able to seduce Job directly into committing the planned sin; but in the Job poem, Job is drawn deeply into a revolt against God which borders on blasphemy, another factor showing the theological connection between the Satan of the folktale and the Job of the poem. Moreover, Job's wife plays the same part as Satan. She speaks to Job the words that exactly express Satan's secret intentions: "Curse God and die." Here is another striking parallel to the serpent and Eve in the Paradise story, as has been mentioned above (see p. 50).

If we consider all this in relation to the nature of the *benē*

70. Wisd. of Sol. 2:24.

hā-'elōhīm, we find that their most distinguishing feature is their belonging to God, in the positive as well as the negative sense. They belong to his total nature; they form his court. But there is apparent in the *benē hā-'elōhīm* the germ of a will of their own; a slight rift starts in God's personality, which loosens the old "seams" and shows us that this unity arose out of an original multiplicity. In other words, behind the self-will of the *benē hā-'elōhīm* the once subjugated will of the old gods is coming alive again. This also becomes clear in the passage, otherwise hard to explain, in Isa. 24:21–23, the so-called "Isaiah Apocalypse": [71]

> And it shall come to pass in that day, that Yahweh shall punish the host of the high ones that are on high, and the kings of the earth upon the earth. And they shall be gathered together, as prisoners are gathered in the pit, and shall be shut up in the prison, and after many days shall they be visited. Then the moon shall be confounded, and the sun ashamed, when the Lord of hosts [*Yahweh ṣebā'ōt*] shall reign in mount Zion, and in Jerusalem, and before his ancients gloriously.

Here both elements must be recognized: the polemic against the ancient astral divinities, but at the same time the punishment of the revolutionary *benē hā-'elōhīm.* Johann Lindblom holds these verses to be a later addition inserted into the Isaiah Apocalypse. This passage, he says, "is obviously connected with late Jewish angelological and eschatological ideas. The best commentary is given us by the Book of Enoch." [72] This reference to a considerably later book can scarcely serve as a valid explanation. A very interesting attempt is made by Julian Morgenstern [73] to show a direct connection between Psalm 82 and our passage, as well as with

71. Joh. Lindblom (*Die Jesaja-Apokalypse* [Lund, 1938], p. 84) places it in the fifth century B.C.; Bernhard Duhm (*Das Buch Jesaja* [1914], pp. 147–48), in the second century B.C.

72. Lindblom, *op. cit.*, p. 27. He refers in particular to En. 90:24, 88; 91:15, 54; etc.

73. *Op. cit.*, pp. 29–126.

Gen. 6:1–4 and Isa. 14:12: "How art thou fallen from Heaven, O Lucifer!" [74] In brief his result is as follows: Ps. 82:6–7—"I have said, Ye are gods; and all of you are children of the most High. But ye shall die like men . . ."—throws a revealing light on Gen. 6:4. We have here a myth of angels who united with the daughters of men and were punished for it by their very "living like men" from then on. Consequently, according to Morgenstern, originally it was not mankind who was punished in Gen. 6:1–4 but the *benē hā-'elōhīm.*[75] In the following phrase in Ps. 82:7, "[ye shall] fall like one of the princes," a further myth is disclosed, that of the rebellious *hēlēl ben šāḥar,* who, because of his rebellion, was cast down.[76] In Isa.

74. This, too, is a later inserted passage, not stemming from Isaiah. B. Duhm (*Das Buch Jesaja,* p. XIII) places it in the second to first century B.C., Julian Morgenstern (*op. cit.,* p. 110, n. 144) between 486 and 476 B.C.

75. That, however, the version as we have it, i.e., the punishment of men, is also not without meaning, I have tried to show above (pp. 112 f.).

76. According to B. Duhm (*Das Buch Jesaja,* p. 96), "an astral fable about Mercury, the Greek legend of Phaëthon, plays a part here, according to which Mercury wanted to climb into heaven with the sun but (because he suddenly became invisible) was turned back." See also Gunkel (*Schöpfung und Chaos* [1895], pp. 133–34): "The morning star, the son of the dawn, has a peculiar fate. Brightly shining he speeds toward heaven, but he does not reach the height; the sun's rays make him fade. This natural process the myth pictures as a battle of 'Eljon against Hêlal, who once wanted to reach the height of heaven but had to go down to the underworld. Very similarly the Greek myth speaks of the early death of Phaëthon, son of Eos; Phaëthon, too, is the morning star; *φαέθων* in its literary meaning is identical to *hēlēl* (shining)." This linguistic derivation, i.e., the translation by "morning star" (in view of all the associated meanings in which the concept is embedded), has much more in its favor than that by "moon," which is supported solely by the Arabic *hilāl* = "new-moon crescent." Cf. Zimmern in Schrader, *KAT,* p. 565, n. 7, referring to Winckler, *Geschichte Israels* (1895), II, 24; *idem, Altorientalische Forschungen* (1898), II, 388; Wellhausen, *Prolegomena zur Geschichte Israels* (4th ed., 1895), p. 111, n. 2. Also Gesenius-Buhl joins in this assumption. That Zimmern feels it necessary to assume in Isaiah 14 the *waning* moon, "whereby the addition *ben šaḥar,* as also the thought of Hêlal's death, would be much better explained," only shows the difficulty of his point of view even more. W. Baumgartner ("Israelitisch-griechische Sagenbeziehungen," *Schweizerisches Archiv für Volkskunde* [1944], pp. 11 f.) draws attention, especially in reference to an analogous North American myth, to

14:12 ff. it appears as the image of the arrogant King of Babylon. Morgenstern believes that Isa. 24:21–24 also relates to one of these myths, or to both of them.[77]

---

the universal character of this motif, and therefore doubts the direct identification of Hêlal and Phaëthon.

A similar myth also appears in Ezek. 28:11–19, applied to the King of Tyre, who, associated with the protecting cherub, was in Eden on the mountain of God and then was cast down to earth because of his presumption. On the question of the origin of this myth, Gunkel says (*Schöpfung und Chaos,* p. 134): "In Babylonian there is so far no evidence of the name Hêlal and the Hêlal myth. However, this does not exclude a Babylonian origin. If Babylonian, the myth would probably relate to Mercury. If not, one would perhaps look for a Phoenician source."

The excavations at Ras Shamra have since thrown more light on the problem. Julian Morgenstern mentions that the figure of "Shahar" appears already in the mythological literature of Ugarit as the son of El and twin brother of Shalem. He refers to the myth, "The Birth of the Gracious and Beautiful Gods," 1, 51, in Montgomery and Harris, *The Ras Shamra Mythological Texts* (1935), 38, 177, and in other places. In W. Baumgartner ("Ras Schamra und das Alte Testament," *Theologische Rundschau* [1940–41], Nos. 3–4, p. 90) we find the more precise statement that there is evidence for a divine pair, "Dawn" and "Sunset" (*šhr* and *šlm*) in the Ugaritic pantheon as early as the second millennium B.C.

77. Starting from B. Duhm's assumption (*Das Buch Jesaja,* pp. 147 f.) that Isaiah 24–27 dates from the second century B.C., Erik Stave (*op. cit.,* p. 191) derives the motif of the fall of the angels from the Persian conception, according to which the evil spirits are cast down at the end of the world. He refers (p. 176) to Bundehesh 3, 26 (*Sacred Books of the East,* ed. F. Max Müller [Oxford, 1895], V, 19): "And ninety days and nights the heavenly angels were contending in the world with the confederate demons of the evil spirit, and hurled them confounded to hell; and the rampart of the sky was formed so that the adversary should not be able to mingle with it." Stave also understands the passage in Isa. 27:1, where the overcoming of the Leviathan and the Tannin seems to be removed into the future, as eschatological in the Parsistic sense.

Both mythologems, however—that of the fall of the angels and that of the overcoming of the sea monster—are of much older origin, the former (see above, n. 76) being evidenced in the Ugaritic, the latter going back to the Marduk myth. In the latter, the different strata of foreign influences upon biblical conceptions become especially clear: in a later time the ancient Canaanite-Babylonian mythologems become a suitable image for the eschatological end fight between God and devil, which for its part shows Persian influence. In the New Testament Satan of Revelation, the identification of the Old Dragon with

Morgenstern's work, however, though extremely valuable for the wide range of material and literature with which he deals, suffers somewhat from the fact that he has drawn many of his conclusions in regard to these inner connections from later versions of the relevant myths found in apocryphal writings. He does say expressly, however, that

> nowhere in the biblical literature has Satan come as yet to play the role which we find attributed to him in the form of the myth recorded in the apocalyptic and N.T. writings, viz., that of the rebellious angel of high rank who seeks to supplant God as the ruler of the universe. . . . Unquestionably the identification of Satan with *Helel ben Shahar* took place only after the period of the Chronicler, i.e., speaking generally, at some time during the third century B.C., and more probably during the second rather than during the first half of the century.[78]

What is significant in our context is that the rebelling astral deities of an ancient myth have, in the Old Testament, become (self-willed) aspects of the one divine personality of Yahweh. As one of the *benē hā-'elōhīm*, the Satan of the Old Testament is related to the mythological background of these passages. It therefore might not be going too far to see in them the real germ cells of the later concept of Satan as the fallen Lucifer.[79] The "Luciferian" quality, as may already

---

Satan is found *expressis verbis*. The battle between Michael and his angels on the one side and the dragon and his angels on the other ends with "the dragon, that old serpent, which is the Devil, and Satan" (20:2) being cast down to earth, in a close parallel, as we may agree with Stave, to the Persian Angro Mainyu, to whom the same thing happens in his unsuccessful attempt to penetrate into the closest entourage of Ahura Mazda (Stave, *op. cit.*, p. 199; see Bundehesh, 3, 10, *Sacred Books of the East*, ed. F. Max Müller [1895], V, 17, cited in another connection below, p. 159, n. 26). Here, in Rev. 20:1–3, the concept hinted at in Isa. 24:21–23 finds its full development.

78. Morgenstern, *op. cit.*, p. 110.

79. The translation of *hēlēl ben šāhar* with "Lucifer" in Isa. 14:12 goes back to the Vulgate. The identification of Satan with the "Lucifer" of Isaiah 14 by Tertullian and Gregory the Great, based on the comparison with Luke 10:18, is therefore an error only from the *historical* point of view; *psychologically* it should be evaluated as a genuine intuition.

have become apparent and will become still clearer in what follows, was already inherent in the nature of the Old Testament Satan.

4. *Satan as One of the* benē hā-'elōhīm *in the Book of Job (1:6–12 and 2:1–7)*

If, from the background of the picture just gained of the *benē hā-'elōhīm*, we turn our eyes to the distinctive meaning which this concept has in the Book of Job, it is not difficult to see that in this story it has undergone a further differentiation. The *benē hā-'elōhīm* are no longer an undivided multiplicity; one among them, Satan, is entrusted with a particular function.[80] This has been met with already in I Kings 22. There, however, it is a matter of an ad hoc commission, while

80. Kaupel's remark (*op. cit.*, p. 96) that in Job 1:6–12 and 2:1–7 Satan appears merely *among* the angels, hence is himself no angel, is too ingenious to be considered. The writer avoids coming to terms with the equally indubitable and painful fact of Satan's presence at the heavenly court by taking refuge in the argument of "poetic language," which says nothing whatever. According to him, this is also what, in Zech. 3:1 ff., makes it possible "to let Satan stay in the proximity of God" *ibid.*, p. 100). Similarly, Erik Stave (*op. cit.*, p. 251) assumes that Satan does not belong "in his inner being" to the *benē hā-'elōhīm*, but only in that he is subject to God and dependent on him. On *betōk* in this passage, cf., in opposition to his view, Driver and Gray, *A Critical and Exegetical Commentary on the Book of Job* ("International Critical Commentary" series) (Edinburgh, 1921), p. 11: "*betōk* is not infrequently tantamount to: (one) of the number of, with others of the *same* class; see Gen. 23:10; 42:5; Num. 17:21; 26:62; I Sam. 10:10; Ezek. 29:12. But as in several of the passages just cited the person or persons in question are peculiar or pre-eminent in the class to which they are referred, so is the Satan here; he is one of the sons of the gods, or angels, and as such subject to and under the control of Yahweh, and incapable of acting beyond the terms of Yahweh's permission; but there are perhaps germs of the later idea of Satan, the opponent of God, dividing with him the allegiance of men (Wisd. 2:24), in the freedom with which he moves about in the earth, so that Yahweh asks where he has been (1:7; 2:2), in contrast to the angels who are *sent* to definite persons and places." Driver and Gray, therefore, from a quite different, linguistic starting point, arrive at the conclusion of a certain independence of Satan vis-à-vis God. This, however, as I tried to show in the foregoing, is already contained in the character of the *benē hā-'elōhīm*. In Satan this independence merely became fully visible.

here Satan's function is already defined by his name. But the important difference is that his own will, unlike that of the "spirit" in the vision of Micaiah ben Imlah, consists not merely in a decision about carrying out a plan of God but apparently in opposing the will of God. He discusses with God, and argues with him, and his arguments affect God. If we go back to what was established about the relation of the *benē hā-'elōhīm* to God, namely, that they are the multiplicity of the aspects of his being which are beginning to manifest themselves as such, the question arises: What side of God's being is embodied in Satan as one of the *benē hā-'elōhīm?* He is not merely a tool of the divine will, even though one aware of itself like the "spirit" in I Kings 22. He embodies a side of Yahweh which, like the "spirit," belongs to him, yet is conscious of himself and known to God not only when called upon. Here one of the *benē hā-'elōhīm* has become more autonomous; he is still more individual. He is an independently active side of God, who is in conflict with God's total personality, and by whose opposing will God is perturbed. God accepts this side of himself and lets it have its way; yet he is critical and uncertain about it. He gives way to it and at the same time restricts it. His acceptance of this side consists first of all in the fact that Satan is assigned a definite task: He roams around on the earth as God's "overseer" of men (on this conception, see below, pp. 134 ff.). This very office is born of suspicion; it is the *'ēl qannā'*—the jealous God of Exodus,[81] who is jealously watching the people whom he has chosen for his own to see if they are his in the way he demands. But here we meet with a changed, more abysmal atmosphere. Whereas elsewhere in the Old Testament God demands unbroken piety and flames into wrath only when he does not meet with it, here Job's obedience does not satisfy him. There lurks in him a secret doubt which in Satan, the separated side of his being, is manifested fully. This whole pattern of interrelations as an inner-divine process comes out beautifully in the details

81. See Exod. 20:5; 34:14.

of the text. Thus, for instance, Satan does not accuse Job on his own incentive, but Yahweh provokes him by an insistent emphasis on Job's piety. It is here that his secret doubt comes to light. He believes, yet does not believe, in Job's piety, for he needs to have it confirmed. The fact that he puts the question, and its provocative form, can be reduced to the basic meaning: Is Job really pious? And Satan's answer is like a voicing of God's suspicion. *Satan appears here as the manifested doubt of God.* He devaluates Job's piety and causes God to deliver Job up to him. That means that God has succumbed to his doubt. There is no way to avoid this conclusion. To be sure, Satan is not autonomous insofar as God agrees to the destruction of Job's happiness. Naturally, in itself it would be conceivable that Satan would act on his own, without regard to Yahweh. But that would mean the complete tearing-apart of God's personality, a total falling-asunder. Moreover, Satan would have destroyed Job's life and therewith God's creation. In other words, God's doubt of his creation would have won, manifested in a destruction of his creation, and therewith, to speak figuratively, would have led to God's self-destruction. That the Old Testament God was subject to such impulses is shown by the story of the Flood; and that he was not immune to them even after the act of grace he bestowed on Noah, in whom he saved the germ of the new world, is shown in the covenant he makes with Noah. He binds himself never again to annihilate mankind, and he sets up a sign of the convenant to remind *himself*, too! For it says expressly:

> And *I* will remember my covenant, which is between me and you and every living creature of all flesh; and the waters shall no more become a flood to destroy all flesh. And the bow shall be in the cloud; and *I will look upon it, that I may remember the everlasting covenant* between God and every living creature of all flesh that is upon the earth.[82]

82. Gen. 9:15, 16 (italics added). That this sign has to do with the rainbow rather than the crescent, as is often accounted a possibility,

The temptation of Abraham also belongs in this context. It must be realized that God risks his whole plan of salvation, and with it his creation, in order to assure himself of Abraham's piety. For Abraham was the carrier of salvation; with him God had made a covenant (Genesis 15); to him he had promised a son of his body and seed innumerable as the stars. And God sealed this covenant with an archaic ritual. He passed as a burning torch between the halves of slain animals which he had previously commanded Abraham to cut in two and subjected himself to the meaning of the archaic rite: Just

seems to me to follow out of this psychological situation. For the rainbow is a *connection* between heaven and earth, God and man. It is really a symbol of the relationship, of the covenant. It is, moreover, not a regular occurrence, which as such would not be very suitable as a symbol of remembrance. Beyond that, the rainbow usually appears after a storm, that is, a divine impulse of wrath which carries in it the danger of destruction. Here it is God who has need of the symbol of remembrance, of the promise which he has given to man! But even if one assumes, like A. Jeremias (*op. cit.*, p. 155), that the "sign" originally was the sickle of the new moon, a "state of war" between Yahweh and his people would be presupposed. Jeremias refers to the Babylonian conception of the new moon as the weapon of the divinity revealing itself in the moon (Virolleaud, *L'Astrologie chaldéenne* [1905], 2d Suppl., VI, 7: *kaštu*ⁱˡ *Sin*), and to the pre-Islamic Arabs, who said of Kuzah that he shoots arrows and after the battle hangs his bow in the clouds. It is interesting in our context that according to Tabarī (Tafsīr) Kuzah's bow later came to be called the bow of *Shaitan* (*Handwörterbuch des Islam, s.v.* "Shaitan," p. 671). Thus, the "state of war" between Yahweh and his people would be closely associated with the darkness of the new moon, which would fit well with the catastrophe of the Flood, and which can be looked at psychologically as the extinguishing of consciousness; on the other hand, this would remain the only "moon trait" of the Old Testament God, to whom elsewhere a fiery nature is ascribed much more frequently. Jeremias thinks, by the way, of a very early change-over of the image of the moon sickle into that of the rainbow. He thinks it possible that the redactor already may have effected the change from war bow to rainbow that came after the Flood (*op. cit.*, p. 270). Significant above all is his mention that the Arabs, too, in connection with their arrow-shooting Kuzah, no longer think of the moon crescent but of the iris (*loc. cit.*). In any case, the rainbow conception gains further support from the fact that the Old Testament contains nothing corresponding to the Babylonian *kaštu*ⁱˡ *Sin;* the new moon is consistently called *ḥōdeš*, while the bow in the clouds (*qešet be-ʿānān*) finds a parallel in Ezek. 1:28, where it unquestionably has to do with the rainbow (*be-yōm hag-gešem*).

as these animals were cut apart, so shall it happen unto me if I break the covenant. Here it may well be said that God—expressed in the image of human psychology in which he appears here symbolically—is staking his own life along with the life of Isaac. Here God's doubt, as it were, already goes to the roots of his own existence. Again the religious instinct of earlier times is shown when a Talmudic legend (Synh. 89b [83]) and even earlier the Jubilees (chapter 18) relate that Satan (called *Mastema* in the Jubilees) persuaded God to test Abraham.[84] The inner relation to the story of Job is evident, yet there is an essential difference. It is to some extent a question of different stages, different "standpoints" of God. With Abraham, as with Noah, it has to do with the inception of the divine plan of creation and redemption. It is, in a way, natural that there should be some uncertainty. There is as yet no tradition of adherence to Yahweh. But against the background of the revelation on Sinai and the people's experience of God in its history up to the time of the poet of the Book of Job,[85] God's doubt appears in another light, all the more since

83. See A. Kohut, *Ueber die jüdische Angelologie und Dämonologie in ihrer Abhängigkeit vom Parsismus* (1866), p. 67.

84. See Erik Stave, *op. cit.*, p. 267. In the same way the Jubilees ascribe to Mastema God's threat to Moses (Exod. 4:24–26), the magic of the Egyptian magicians, the hardening of the Egyptians, and the slaying of the firstborn of Egypt (*ibid.*, n. 1).

85. That *his* time, not the ancient time in which the Job poet sets his story, can alone determine its theological interpretation seems self-evident to me. Torczyner's view, that we have here to do with a conversion story, in which Yahweh reveals himself to a "heathen," an Edomite ("Hiobdichtung und Hiobsage," *Monatsschrift für Geschichte und Wissenschaft des Judentums* [1925], pp. 234–48), does not seem convincing, since it is just in the framing story, which contains the reference to Edom and the archaic period (sacrifice), that the divine name of Yahweh appears. Moreover, Job's speeches are so permeated with the knowledge of the ambivalent personality of God that, solely from the inner motivation, they cannot proceed from a "novice." His experience of God is far too differentiated for that, as will be shown later. Nevertheless, there seems to me to be something true in Torczyner's view: we are dealing here with a "conversion" to a new attitude toward God and with it a change and further development of the Yahweh religion.

In regard to the relationship of the Israelite and Edomite body of

Job fulfills the standard of piety valid up to that time. Therefore the doubt cannot refer to an existing situation but is connected with a claim of God which only becomes apparent through the events induced by Satan's doubt. For by God's doubt becoming manifest in Satan, and its effects on man, God, too, is changed, as I shall try to show. This change is the main issue. It is the driving force behind the doubt, it causes God to submit to the doubt; he *must* submit to it, for his own sake. The doubt here lies much deeper than in the story of Abraham's sacrifice. There it was to some extent justified. Abraham had not yet proved himself. Only afterward does God say: "Lay not thine hand upon the lad, neither do thou anything unto him: *for now I know* that thou fearest God" (Gen. 22:12; italics added). But about Job, he really knows from the outset that he is obedient (Job 1:8); the doubt is apparently without grounds, yet God has to submit to it, so to speak, as a matter of fate, in order to experience himself. So Satan is the destructive doubt within God's personality; yet it has a mysterious existential necessity for God and man and their relation to each other. That all this happens—even though as yet incomprehensibly—because God needs man, because he is drawn to man, is expressed in a deep presentiment of Job's when he says:

> Oh that thou wouldest hide me in the grave, that thou wouldest keep me secret, until thy wrath be past, that thou wouldest appoint me a set time, and remember me! . . . all the days of my appointed time will I wait, till my change come. Thou shalt call, and I will answer thee: *thou wilt have a desire to the work of thine hands.*[86]

---

traditions in our story, Joh. Lindblom's view (*La composition du livre de Job* [Lund, 1945]), for which he gives detailed evidence, seems to me to have much in its favor (the summary of his textual criticism is on p. 29). "The legend of Job is of Edomite origin but was later transmitted to Palestine; there it was transformed in conformity with the spirit of the Yahweh religion, and became the foundation of the considerable work which we call today the Book of Job. The foreign work received an Israelite imprint. The Edomite Sheikh became a biblical patriarch" (p. 6).

86. Job 14:13–15; italics added.

Sellin cites this passage and speaks of the "bold thought of God's longing love for the pious man."[87] This "bold thought," however, did not spring from the head but from the heart, as a living religious experience of deepest content.

Now what is the change brought about by Satan, who is the activated doubt of God? This must be traced in the details of the text. Here it becomes absolutely necessary to see the framing story and the poem as a whole, as was mentioned before. But how can we solve the problem of the considerable difficulties the text presents, which oppose such a view? In the extensive literature on the subject the inconsistencies between the framing story and the poem have been pointed out repeatedly, in particular the most significant one: that Job, the patient sufferer of the framing story, cannot be the impatient and rebellious Job of the poem. As has been said (see above, p. 97), Sellin's idea of the text seems to me to be the most tenable. According to him, the author of the Book of Job used an old folktale of the pious Job and worked it into his poem. But this amalgamation was not carried through in every section. The folktale, with its altogether different point, was left in its entirety. Is it not possible to assume that it was known to the author and inspired him to transform it according to his own different religious situation? Sellin believes above all (as was mentioned above; see pp. 96 f.) that the Satan passages in chapters 1 and 2 did not belong to the original story, for otherwise God's victory over Satan would surely have been mentioned. But in connection with the poem this circumstance can be explained. Satan is the instigator; but in the end it is by no means any longer a primitive "either/or" situation of a victory of God or Satan. By means of Satan something new has come to pass; a new plane of inner happenings has been reached within God and thus also within man. Looked at from the point of view of the whole drama, Satan is needed to give full expression to the divine impulse which has set the whole process in motion.

87. Sellin, *op. cit.* (n. 42, above), p. 9.

If one reads the framing story from Sellin's point of view, without the Satan passages, the result is actually a closed tale of a pious man who is afflicted and yet never wavers in his loyalty to God. For this he is then richly rewarded by God.

Sellin's theory also receives strong support from the fact that all the blows directed against Job, except the last one, are carried out by God himself. If the Satan passage (1:6–12) belonged to the folktale, it would seem very striking that, in verse 12, God delivers Job into Satan's hands and Satan departs to carry out his work of destruction, as one would assume. But then, in what follows, there is no mention that it is Satan who deals the blows. It is people, lightning (the fire of God!), and storm which destroy the happiness of Job's life (cf., above, pp. 84 f.). Several Old Testament parallels show that the last plague also, Job's boils, the only one coming from Satan, could just as well have stemmed from God. The same bad boils appear in Exod. 9:9 as a plague sent by God through Moses upon the Egyptians. And *ṣāra'at*, the word for leprosy, according to Gesenius-Buhl literally means "blow, scourge of God" (from *ṣāra'*, "knocking down"), because leprosy was regarded as a punishment from God—his blows, as it were.[88] Several passages testify that God also sends pestilence; e.g., Exod. 9:3 (blow against the Egyptians), Lev. 26:25; Deut. 28:21.[89]

The Epilogue, too, according to Sellin,[90] was obviously connected to the poem subsequently. The three friends introduced by the author (2:11–13) are mentioned again in 42:7–9. But the "seam" is easy to see. In Sellin's view, which seems convincing to me, verse 10 of chapter 42 followed immediately after 2:10 in the old folktale: "In all this did not Job sin with his lips." Then, "And Yahweh turned the captivity of Job. . . ."

88. See Num. 12:10: the punishment of Miriam with leprosy.

89. Looked at in the light of these passages, Sellin's view that Satan represents an unburdening of God from evil is shown to be, in any case, premature as far as Satan in the Book of Job is concerned (cf. above, p. 97).

90. *Op. cit.*, pp. 24 f.

How this folktale, complete in itself, came to be united with the poem can probably no longer be determined. Nevertheless, Sellin's statement of the inner connection of the Satan concept with the poem seems decisive to me, and the fact that they appear interwoven, yet each still distinguishable from the other, seems to express precisely the transition from one attitude to the other.

Job of the folktale knows nothing about Satan. He unproblematically accepts all blows as coming from God. He finds it, so to speak, quite in order that God should take everything away from him: " . . . shall we receive good at the hand of God, and shall we not receive evil?" (2:10). Not so the Job of the poem. He rebels. And he experiences the falling-apart of the two sides of God. *God splits apart in him.* Satan does not appear to Job as such; all the events having to do with Satan take place in heaven, in the circle of the *benē hā-'elōhīm.* It is an issue between divine beings, between God and Satan. But the *reflex,* as it were, in the human realm is the split of the God image in Job: God is no longer accepted unquestioningly in his ambivalence; rather, this ambivalence is manifested as such to Job through his experience. Job becomes conscious of it, just as God, on the heavenly plane, becomes conscious of his own doubt when it opposes him. It is really one identical process, in its divine and its human manifestations.

It is in the most pointed way, in the sharpest paradox, that Job experiences the duality of God in his unity, the process in God that is consummated mythologically with Satan's separation from the "divine beings." These are Job's words (16:20, 21): ". . . mine eye poureth out tears unto God. O that one might *plead for a man with God . . .*" (italics added). And 17:3: "Lay down now, put me in a surety with thee; . . ."

Job is sure of his "witness in heaven" (16:19) and at the same time feels the uncanny awesomeness of the divine urge toward destruction. He, the human being, reminds God that in him he will be destroying his own creation (10:8–9): "Thine hands have made me and fashioned me together round about; yet thou dost destroy me. *Remember*, I beseech thee, that thou hast made me as the clay; and wilt thou bring me into dust again?" (Italics added.)

Job feels how monstrous the situation is, and he can no longer accept it. He is beyond the naïveté of Abraham, who obeyed without question. Job feels responsible for himself as a created being and lays hold of God's arm, who is about to destroy his own creation. He is not able to endure this aspect of God. It is not possible for him until the process within God himself has reached a further stage. One must therefore ask: What effect did Satan have upon God? Only by submitting to his dark side in the conflict is God able to grasp its nature. God consciously experiences his own unpredictability. He not only *is* it; he knows about it. It is in this totality that he wants to be apprehended by man. So he manifests himself to Job in his terrible aspect of the power of nature. God experiences his dark nature side in the tremendous images of Leviathan and Behemoth.[91] He is aware of his own cruelty: "Will he [the crocodile] make many supplications unto thee? Will he speak soft words unto thee?" (41:3). And in terrifying self-irony he goes on: "Will he make a covenant with thee? Wilt thou take him for a servant for ever?" (41:4).

Here the God of the covenant mocks the contract. He is not the slave of man by the covenant he made with him. He can do otherwise, too. He is also the dark nature god who can destroy what he has created. It might be argued that God has always been aware of his dark side. Many times he threatens wrath and annihilation. He even experiences fear of himself when he says to Moses (Exod. 33:3): "For I will not go up in

91. I do not want to enter here into the problem of literary criticism as to whether or not these words of God are interpolations, because it seems to me irrelevant in this context. Rudolf Otto (*The Idea of the Holy*, trans. John W. Harvey [New York, 1958]) expresses the essential when he writes: "It is conjectured that the descriptions of the hippopotamus (Behemoth) and the crocodile (Leviathan) in XL:15 ff. are a later interpolation. This may well be the fact; but if so, it must be admitted that the interpolator felt the point of the entire section extraordinarily well."

the midst of thee; for thou art a stiffnecked people: lest I consume thee in the way." Volz comments very pertinently: "So Yahweh would preferably avoid meeting his own demonic nature; he is able to keep away from the cause of an outburst of wrath, but he has no control over the outburst itself." [92] However, here and in other passages God's unpredictability is simply a given fact, not a problem. In God's speeches to Job it is a problem, insofar as God consciously admits it, acknowledges the darkness in himself, and wants to be accepted with it by man. And Job does so accept him because he has seen him, because God has revealed himself to him anew. He no longer demands his rights; he bows to the irrational God. "I have heard of thee by the hearing of the ear: *but now mine eye seeth thee*. Wherefore I abhor myself and repent in dust and ashes" (42:5, 6; italics added).

Sellin, in spite of his important factual discoveries, proceeds from wrong theological assumptions which lead to a misunderstanding of the end of the book. He holds the "capitulation" of Job to be totally incomprehensible after his previous "revolution," and suggests that the author of Job inserted this speech of God many years later, in his resigned old age.[93] In contrast, Rudolf Otto has a beautiful and profound conception of this passage:

> That is an admission of inward *convincement* and conviction, not of impotent collapse and submission to merely superior power. Nor is there here at all the frame of mind to which St. Paul now and then gives utterance; e.g., Rom. IX:20: "Shall the thing formed say to him that formed it, Why hast thou made me thus? Hath not the potter power over the clay, of the same lump to make one vessel unto honour, and another unto dishonour?" To interpret the passage in Job thus would be a misunderstanding of it. This chapter does not proclaim, as Paul does, the renunciation of, the realization of the impossibility of, a "theo-

92. Volz, *Das Dämonische in Jahwe*, p. 33.
93. Sellin, *op. cit.*, p. 39.

> dicy"; rather, it aims at putting forward a real theodicy of its own, and a better one than that of Job's friends; a theodicy able to convict even a Job, and not only to convict him, but utterly to still every inward doubt that assailed his soul. For latent in the weird experience that Job underwent in the revelation of Elohim is at once an inward relaxing of his soul's anguish and an appeasement, an appeasement which would alone and in itself perfectly suffice as the solution of the problem of the Book of Job, even without Job's rehabilitation in Chapter XLII, where recovered prosperity comes as an extra payment thrown in after quittance has been already rendered.[94]

The nature of this satisfaction first became really clear to me only through an illuminating comment of C. G. Jung: In his great final speech God reveals himself to Job in all his frightfulness. It is as if he said to Job: "Look, that's what I am like. That is why I treated you like this." Through the suffering which he inflicted upon Job out of his own nature, God has come to this self-knowledge and admits, as it were, this knowledge of his frightfulness to Job. *And that is what redeems the man Job.* This is really the solution to the enigma of Job, that is, a true justification for Job's fate, which, without this background, would, in its cruelty and injustice, remain an open problem. Job appears here clearly as a sacrifice, but also as the carrier of the divine fate, and that gives meaning to his suffering and liberation to his soul.

This thought is further supported by the fact that in his speech God represents himself as the union of the opposite duality of Leviathan and Behemoth; for Leviathan is a sea animal, and Behemoth a land animal. In later apocryphal writings this opposition comes to light even more: In the Ethiopian Book of Enoch, 60:7–8 (about second to first century B.C.) they are spoken of as the female Leviathan of the sea and the male Behemoth of the wilderness, who are divided up at the end of days and served to the pious as a eucharistic

94. R. Otto, *op. cit.*, p. 78.

meal of sorts. The same motif is found also in the Syrian Apocalypse of Baruch, 29:4 (about second to third century A.D.). In a certain sense the Book of Job represents an anticipation of the meaning of this symbolism, in that the integration of God as the *coincidentia oppositorum* occurs on *the plane of Job's consciousness.*

Yahweh has revealed himself to Job as an ambivalent divine personality. And Job, wrenched from his satisfied existence of unproblematic piety rewarded with the goods of life, has been transformed into one who accepts not only the good God, but also the dark one, and so comes to a much deeper certainty: "I know that my redeemer liveth." Otto, in my opinion, is absolutely right in seeing this inner change in Job, effected by the divine revelation in chapter 38, as the final significance of the poem, compared to which the Epilogue of chapter 42 is an anticlimax. The standpoint of the transformed Job is totally different from that of chapter 42. The Epilogue is the other half of the shell out of which grew the poem proper, *with* the concept of Satan. The original folktale is actually only the shell, which is stripped off again.

If we now look back to ask what role Satan has played in this work of transformation, we find that, by means of the doubt concerning Job, he is the *spiritus agens* of this change; but he is also the destructive activity of God arising out of God's doubt of man. As Satan, God destroys the man whom he cannot use, whom he cannot trust, without its being clear *why* he mistrusts him or for what he needs him. This "why" and "what for," however, are closely connected. They must have to do with some divine intention or inclination which is already at work, though not yet apparent. At the end Job is inwardly "expanded"; he is able to comprehend an experience of God which, if he still had been the simple, unproblematic, pious Job, and if Satan had not driven him to come to terms with the *deus absconditus,* would probably have split him apart. One must therefore assume that it was this being comprehended, this having room in man, which was important for God. He obviously wants man to be the carrier of his (divine) self-knowledge. This high dignity of man is shown in the unexpressed demands of God on him, which incite God to such a passionate self-revelation. The paradoxical depth of God's speech in chapter 38 becomes fully evident only when it is seen that this God, who is so passionately wooing man, does so by describing to man his world-wide superiority as the power of nature. Man is nothing over against this tremendous divine force, yet God needs him in order to *know* this power. God needs man for the sake of insight. Perhaps even the old Messianic, prophetic passage, Isa. 11:1–11, belongs in this same context. It describes a Messianic figure endowed with spiritual and ethical qualities. "And the spirit of the Lord shall rest upon him, the spirit of wisdom and understanding, the spirit of counsel and might, the spirit of knowledge and of the fear of Yahweh" (Isa. 11:2). "They shall not hurt nor destroy in all my holy mountain: for the earth shall be full of the *knowledge of Yahweh*, as the waters cover the sea" (11:9; italics added). Is it not, in a way, also a *divine* longing and need for redemption that speaks in these words?

In the Book of Job God has, psychologically speaking, advanced a long step further than in the story of Paradise, where he still knows so little why he created mankind that he casts them away from him because of their knowledge of good and evil. Here one can begin to sense that man's knowing about good and evil is what really matters. Here Satan brought it about, there the serpent—another "evil" idea of God's. It becomes clear, however, that this knowledge is fruitful only when coupled with submission to God; otherwise it turns to a hybrid "godlikeness." In this connection it becomes profoundly significant that in Job Satan acts in agreement with God, not "behind his back" like the serpent in Paradise.

If we now ask ourselves how Satan's function in this story can be connected with what we have learned of him up to now, it may be said that his function in the Book of Job is a further development of the functional concept he expresses. He appears here in full light, as the metaphysical foe of a peaceful life and worldly comfort. He intervenes as a disturbance and hindrance to the natural order of living and steps in man's way like the *mal'āk Yahweh* as *Satan* in the path of Balaam. However, while the Balaam story concerns the experience of a clash of wills and blind obedience—a first realization, so to speak, that God's will, not one's own, must be fulfilled—in Job's case it is a matter of conscious submission to God's will, born of inner insight. Satan is here truly Lucifer, the bringer of light. He brings man the knowledge of God, but through the suffering he inflicts on him. Satan is the misery of the world which alone drives man inward, into the "other world." It is Satan who drives man beyond himself as animal being, as mere creature of nature. In this very specific sense perhaps the (Mosaic) Law already had something Luciferian and "Satanic." It was, one might say, the first form in which the people of Israel was driven out of a merely natural condition, out of the paradise of animal existence. Torn out of a merely natural state by the revelation on Sinai, it became God's possession; its life was no longer its own, it was not allowed any longer to run its course anonymously, but obtained a meaning and a fate. It was given the impress of God's fate. The Law was to some extent a necessary prior stage before man could become a vessel for God.[95] Job is the pious man who reaches, through suffering, a deeper piety which is capable of enduring God in his light-dark aspect and of surrendering himself to him.

95. The Law as attitude toward God had, in the Old Testament itself, reached a great deepening, as is shown beautifully in Deut. 30:11–14: "For this commandment which I command thee this day, it is not hidden from thee, neither is it far off. It is not in heaven, that thou shouldest say, Who shall go up for us to heaven, and bring it unto us, that we may hear it, and do it? Neither is it beyond the sea, that thou shouldest say, Who shall go over the sea for us, and bring it unto us, that we may hear it, and do it? But the word is very nigh unto thee, in thy mouth, and *in thy heart,* that thou mayest do it." (Italics added.)

5. *Babylonian Traits in the Image of Satan in the Book of Job*

Now that we have tried to answer the essential question of the meaning of Satan in the Old Testament, especially as evidenced in the Book of Job, it still remains to establish what "threads" have been woven into the "basic pattern," what particular traits in the image of Satan in the Book of Job can presumably or surely be ascribed to foreign influence.

As was mentioned earlier (see above, p. 90), the disease-inflicting function of Satan seems to be a reminiscence of the Babylonian demon of sickness. But how peripheral its importance is in the total picture of the Satan in the Book of Job can be seen by a comparison with the aforementioned "Poem of the Righteous Sufferer" (see above, pp. 90 f.), which only now can be carried through fully.

1. In contrast to Satan in the Book of Job, the demon of the Babylonian poem is exclusively a sickness demon. The Old Testament Satan, insofar as he can be called a sickness demon, does not function specifically as such. On the contrary, this function connects him directly with Yahweh himself. It has already been pointed out that at other times Yahweh himself sends sickness (see above, p. 125).

2. In the Babylonian poem the sickness demon is opposed by the good god who overcomes him, while, in the Book of Job, Satan acts with God's permission! This mutual agreement between God and Satan resulting from their confrontation is, in comparison with the Babylonian demon, the new and important factor in the Job Satan. With his doubt of Job and his "tempting" of God, he moves onto a psychological plane which removes him almost beyond any comparison with the demon in the Babylonian poem. The specific factor in the Satan of the Book of Job is his relation to Yahweh, his origin in him, which I have tried to demonstrate by means of the manifold examples of identical functions, as also by his *benē hā-'elōhīm* character.[96]

96. The Babylonian example also makes it very clear that the fact of

3. Perhaps the deepest and most essential difference between the two poems is that in the Babylonian song the king ascribes his suffering to the adversary, while Job ascribes his to God.[97] In the Babylonian conception the dualism of god and demon reach down to the sphere of human consciousness; in the Book of Job the opposites have not split apart the frame of the one divine personality. (In view of the later development one may perhaps say: not yet.) This is probably the most important evidence against the assumption that the Old Testament Satan was "taken over" from Babylon.

However, another trait of the Job Satan is undoubtedly of Babylonian origin, and is shown even more clearly in Zechariah: that is his *character as accuser*. According to the Babylonian conception, the "accuser" was the polar opposite of the guardian god. According to Zimmern,[98] the idea of a special divine guardian (*il amêli* = "god of man") and of a guardian goddess (*ištar amêli* = "goddess of man") was strongly developed in Babylon. This special guardian god and the guardian goddess of a person intercede with the great gods. In the same way, every individual has an "accuser" (*bêl dabâbi*) and an "accuser goddess" (*bêlit dabâbi*), "persecutor," and so forth.[99] In the Book of Job it is more a matter of the latter nuance:

Satan's subordination to Yahweh, which is generally regarded as specifically inherent in the Old Testament, simply does not discriminate Satan from the Babylonian demon. For, as demon, the latter is also lower than the god.

97. The same difference between the Old Testament Satan and the Persian Ahriman was already stated by M. C. de Harlez ("Satan and Ahriman," *Proceedings of the Society of Biblical Archaeology*, IX, 369): "It would not occur to anyone that Satan could be the cause of these evils. A Mazdean, however, could not hesitate a minute to attribute the origin completely and exclusively to this evil demon. For a sectarian of the Avestas, Angro-Mainyus alone is the author of all evil things, be they moral or physical."

98. In Schrader, *KAT*, pp. 454–55.

99. *Ibid.*, p. 461. (I am indebted to Prof. W. Baumgartner of Basel for pointing out to me the interesting fact that *bēl dabābi* became in Syrian a borrowed term for the accuser and enemy in general [see Brockelmann, *Lexicon Syriacum*[2], p. 83b]; also in Mandaean [see Nöldeke, *Mandäische Grammatik*, 27.151].)

"persecutor, oppressor," less outspokenly of the accuser, although his investigatory rovings imply such an activity. The function of accuser is explicit in Zech. 3:1 ff. It goes back to the Babylonian concept taken from the profane court procedures, according to which "the regulation of the relationship between God and man runs absolutely the same course as that of the ordinary court procedure, where God is the judge and man the seeker for justice." [100] In these court proceedings between God and man, the accuser appears. That this particular development of a Babylonian mythological figure was probably a late acquisition in Yahwism is also shown by the fact that the corresponding idea of the Babylonian guardian god likewise appears very late in the Old Testament in the form of guardian angels; namely, only in Job 5:1 and 33:23 and in Pss. 34:8 and 31:11.

In this period, when the process of differentiation within Yahweh had advanced further, the accuser quality of the Satan figure could easily be assimilated. The restlessly roving oppressor and persecutor of the Babylonian concept becomes an adequate expression of the unrest, suspicion, and doubt *in* Yahweh, as I have tried to show before. This Babylonian characteristic is just what gives the figure of Satan a wider meaning and depth and raises its significance far beyond that of the Babylonian sickness demon.

It is not impossible that the accuser character of Satan, especially in Zech. 3:1 ff., has been influenced in part also by an institution of the Persian court, as has been pointed out especially by Torczyner [101] and Lods.[102] There certain royal officials who traveled about the country were called the "Eyes of the King." Lods, however, draws attention to the fact that the expression "eye of the king" was already used in

100. *Ibid.*, p. 463.

101. H. Torczyner, "How Satan Came into the World," *Expository Times* (1936–37), pp. 563 ff.

102. A. Lods, "Les Origines de la figure de Satan, ses fonctions à la cour céleste," *Mélanges Syriens offerts à M. R. Dussaud* (1939), pp. 565 f.

Medea and Egypt.[103] Yet, what seems to me of the utmost interest regarding our investigation, in which it became evident that the Old Testament Satan has his origin in a process of differentiation within the deity, is Lods's statement that the official entitled the "Eye of the King" was also called "the son" or "the brother of the king." However, this Persian trait, too, would have been ascribed to the Old Testament Satan only as a ready-to-hand symbol for a distinct phase of this very process of divine differentiation.[104]

To summarize, it may be said: The alien influence for which there is any real evidence proves to be late and does not suffice to explain the whole complex of the figure of Satan in the Old Testament. It is a matter of an organically accreted, "accrystalized"[105] trait; but the "entelechy" of the whole appearance must be understood entirely from its connection with the divine personality of Yahweh. The necessity for this approach is expressed symbolically, with all possible plainness, by the *benē hā-'elōhīm* quality of Satan, by his position in heaven, that is, in the inner realm of the godhead.

103. According to Alex. Moret, *Histoire de l'Orient* (Paris, Presses Universitaires, 1936), II, 760.

104. For more complete details on the problem of the possible origin of the Old Testament figure of Satan in the Persian religion, see below, pp. 155 ff.

105. See Gerhard von Rad, art. "διάβολος," in Kittel, *Theologisches Wörterbuch zum Neuen Testament,* II.

Satan as Opponent of the *mal'āk Yahweh* (Zechariah 3:1 ff.)

IN THE FOURTH VISION of Zechariah, Satan appears as the accuser at the right hand of the high priest Joshua:

> And the *mal'āk Yahweh*[1] said unto Satan, Yahweh rebuke thee, O Satan; even Yahweh that hath chosen Jerusalem rebuke thee: is not this a brand plucked out of the fire? Now Joshua was clothed with filthy garments, and stood before the angel. And he answered and spake unto those that stood before him, saying, Take away the filthy garments from him. And to him he said, Behold, I have caused thine iniquity to pass from thee, and I will clothe thee with change of raiment.

The historically conditioned background of the vision is emphasized by J. W. Rothstein.[2] He cites Ewald, who sees the vision as occasioned "by an actual or only threatening accusation at the Persian court." Rothstein himself sees in the procedure of the heavenly accuser a reflected image of a real accusation, or at least a libelous attack against Joshua on earth, in which "the earthly counterpart of the visionary event has, however, a causal connection with the denunciation of the Jewish community to the Persian authorities."[3]

1. The Hebrew text has "*Yahweh*," but another manuscript (Syriaca) has "*mal'āk Yahweh*" (see footnote to Hebrew text in *Biblia Hebraica*, ed. Rudolf Kittel). The Zürich Bible translates correspondingly "Engel des Herrn."
2. *Die Nachtgesichte des Sacharja* (1910), pp. 102 ff.
3. *Ibid.*, p. 107.

Here, as a matter of principle, it should be said that the historical approach to a vision can easily be misleading, insofar as one considers it to be a real vision, as Rothstein also does here.[4] It projects into it conscious reflection, while the vision is a spontaneous revelation of something not known before; that is, of something unconscious. The historical element is merely an image for a new content, just as dreams may be linked to events of the day but are not evoked by them. (Otherwise, how could one explain why, out of the multiplicity of the day's events, just this particular one should emerge in the dream?) Therefore it is already moving in the direction of rationalistic prejudice to speak of the "historical occasion for the vision," as Rothstein does here. Certainly all historical elements are attached to the figure of the high priest Joshua, but the whole scene implies a symbolic and not a concrete significance. It is the nature of a vision to be the image of an inner, not an outer, situation. The fact that only Joshua, not the people, is expressly spoken of is far from proving that "it really is only a matter of Yahweh's witnessing in favor of the priest Joshua personally . . . hence that the accusation which is to be refuted concerns him alone," as Rothstein [5] believes, in agreement with Ewald and others, and in opposition to Baudissin,[6] Marti,[7] and Nowack.[8] What we are really concerned with here is a new religious truth expressing itself in a political vision. It does of course arise out of the situation of the time and is related to it as an answer, but not in an external sense. It is as if the content of the vision coincided with the historical data. Otherwise it would not be a genuine vision but a consciously constructed allegory. Moreover, certain details confirm its symbolic character by their correspondence to other mythical material. Alfred Jere-

4. *Ibid.*, p. 102.
5. *Ibid.*, p. 115.
6. *Geschichte des alttestamentlichen Priestertums* (1889), p. 252.
7. *Das Dodekapropheton* (1904), p. 408. Cf. also *idem*, "Zwei Studien zu Sacharja. I. Der Ursprung des Satans," *Theologische Studien und Kritiken* (1892), p. 210.
8. *Die kleinen Propheten* (1904), p. 353.

mias mentions various parallels to the motif of festive raiment in which Joshua is to be clothed.[9] So the accused Adapa appears before the God of Heaven in mourning clothes and receives a festal garment. The penitent Sumerian king in the song "I will praise the Lord of Wisdom" is cleansed by angels and led through the gates of the heavenly city.[10] Gilgamesh, after being rescued, is cleansed by the hero of the flood on the island of the community of the gods, and so forth.

Karl Marti has made an interesting attempt toward a psychological interpretation of the Satan in Zechariah.[11] He sees in him the carrier of the people's self-accusations, which at that time were a consequence of the law. This figure "is the image of the inner voice projected to the outside, coming up against the grace of God." [12] Marti shows here the right feeling for the spiritual-psychological character of the Old Testament figure of Satan. However, he diminishes the value of his psychological conception, in itself noteworthy, by assuming that Zechariah had himself "created this Satan figure." This is controverted, not only by the whole phenomenology of Satan, the rootedness of this concept in the whole context of the Old Testament theological categories (his angel nature, etc.), but also, above all, by the aforementioned basic psychological fact that inner images are not made, but happen. They are symbols of suprapersonal events in the human soul. So the Satan in Zechariah's vision is not, as Marti assumes, "nothing but the carrier of the accusations, which resulted necessarily from the law at that time," [13] but rather a figure in the suprapersonal *divine* drama, as will become clear in what follows.

9. Alfred Jeremias, *Das Alte Testament im Lichte des alten Orients* (1930), p. 738.
10. This refers to the "Poem of the Righteous Sufferer," which was discussed above. (See H. Gressmann, *Altorientalische Texte zum Alten Testament,* 2d ed. [1926], pp. 278 f.)
11. Marti, "Zwei Studien zu Sacharja. I. Der Ursprung des Satans," pp. 207–45.
12. *Ibid.*, p. 235.
13. *Ibid.*

Satan appears here as the accuser before the court of justice. It is the aforementioned Babylonian trial situation, where the accuser stands on the right of the accused and the defender on the left. He stands before the *mal'āk Yahweh.* If we remember that in the Book of Job Satan stands out among the *benē hā-'elōhīm,* we can see that here there is a polarity expressed by two angelic beings. Satan and the *mal'āk Yahweh,* two angels, *two aspects of God, are fighting over man.* One wants to annihilate him, the other to save him. The opposition is more outspoken than in the Book of Job, where Yahweh's wavering still blurs the boundaries. To be sure, there the wager maintains the opposition, but only in part; for at the bottom, as we have seen, by entering on this wager God has moved to the plane of the "satanic" doubt. He follows it. The opposition is really upheld only by the restrictions on Satan. He is allowed almost to annihilate Job, but not entirely. In Zech. 3:1 ff. the differentiation process has advanced further. *The separation of Satan, the dark side of God, is followed by the corresponding release of God's light side.* The two sides of God's nature are no longer presented in an indistinguishable mixture; they have become discernible as such, and focused on *man.* It is a judgment upon man. Behind it stands the moral demand on the human being, as it also appeared as its last consequence in the Book of Job. This situation provides a definite outline for the character of the two sides. The one wants *justice;* the other grants *mercy.* This seems to me one of the very great turning points in the Old Testament concept of God. Satan becomes what so far has been a positive quality of God, his justice. God's justice literally becomes "devilish."[14] It becomes a hindrance and is

14. Cf. Adolphe Lods, "Les Origines de la figure de Satan, ses fonctions à la cour céleste," *Mélanges Syriens offerts à M. R. Dussaud* (1930), p. 650: "Hence, the *śāṭān* represents here the conscience, the strict law which finds itself, in our case, in opposition to the compassionate intentions of Jahwe, justice fighting with mercy," a deep exegetical insight, from which, however, Lods, in this work primarily directed toward the historical, does not bring out the consequences concerning the *theological* significance of the figure of Satan.

evaluated negatively because a higher principle is visualized: the principle of *love*.[15] Of course the love and compassion of God have been spoken of before, as in Deut. 4:31: "For Yahweh thy God is a merciful God [*'el raḥūm*]; he will not forsake thee, neither destroy thee, nor forget the covenant of thy fathers which he sware unto them." And Ps. 86:15: "But thou, O Yahweh, art a God full of compassion [*'ēl raḥūm we-ḥannūn*], and gracious, long-suffering, and plenteous in mercy and truth." Further, Isa. 54:10: "For the mountains shall depart, and the hills be removed; but my kindness [*ḥasdī*] shall not depart from thee, neither shall the covenant of my peace be removed, saith Yahweh that hath mercy on thee [*me-raḥamēk*]." And Jer. 3:12: ". . . I will not cause mine anger to fall upon you: for I am merciful [*ḥāsīd*], saith Yahweh, and I will not keep anger for ever." But for the most part these are words of *promise*, while our passage presents us with the actual *event* of a merciful and conscious intervention on the part of Yahweh. It is nowhere so conscious as here, where it stands in opposition to its counterpole, justice. This

---

Also Erik Stave (*Ueber den Einfluss des Parsismus auf das Judentum* [Haarlem, 1898], p. 254) finds himself really forced to see in Satan "a personification of the justice of the holy God," but then is unable to maintain the thought because a later concept of Satan gets in his way, namely, that Satan from the beginning appears "as a malicious spirit who shows an inner pleasure and joy in being allowed to cause suffering to men and to entice them to sin." Stave is not able to bridge this seeming contradiction. But to assume it at all leads away from just the essential meaning of this passage. Diestel ("Set-Typhon, Asahel und Satan: Ein Beitrag zur Religionsgeschichte des Orients," *Zeitschrift für die historische Theologie*, XXX, No. 2 [1860], 213) has remarked before this that it would not be justified "to ascribe to the Satan of Job all sorts of evil purposes, wishes, and hopes about which there is no word in the Prologue; this is done unjustifiably in order to bring his figure closer to the New Testament concept; therewith one breaks the law of historical strictness." This can be applied without modification to the consideration of the Satan in Zechariah. The "devilishness" does not consist here in its opposition to justice, but in justice itself.

15. Cf. also Rothstein (*Kommentar zum 1. Buch der Chronik*, ed. D. I. Hänel [1927], p. 380): "As the opposite to Satan, the representative of divine justice . . . the *mal'āk Yahweh* is the carrier of divine mercy and grace . . . ; he is the *hypostatized effectiveness of Jahwe's love, detached from Yahweh's personal being*" (italics added).

is made especially clear in Psalm 86, which has just been cited, where justice and mercy appear side by side. In the Psalm there is no problem in this respect. It could arise only after the dark side had emerged and evoked its opposite. Only here is the negative aspect of justice made manifest. It is solely negative when it *takes the place* of love. And since love can now become manifest, justice becomes the obstacle to be overcome. Justice wants to punish man for his sins. If one imagines what it would have meant if Yahweh had let Satan have his way, one can grasp the "satanic" element in justice. Stave says rightly of this passage: "So here Satan has become the *adversary of God and of the whole plan of salvation.* . . ." [16] Once more it is made very plain that he is the side of God which had already demanded of Abraham the slaying of his only son; for there, too, God is his own adversary, as it were—the opponent of his own plan of salvation.

The Satan in Zechariah's vision demands the *just* punishment of Joshua. But the *mal'āk Yahweh* rescues the "brand plucked out of the fire." Here Yahweh has mastered his dark side.

This thought seems to me to represent the outermost edge of the Old Testament, which can be looked upon as the Old Testament premise for the idea of love in the New Testament. But the thought has also found a highly significant further development in later Judaism, in the Sefiroth tree of the Kabbala.[17] There the totality of spiritual essence is represented in ten spheres, which are levels of emanations of God depicted as the branches of the tree of life, whose roots are above and whose crown is below. In their polar correspondences the nature of the world is expressed in all strata of existence, from the highest to the lowest. Now in this system, mercy or love (*ḥesed*) [18] is placed on the right (masculine)

16. *Ibid.*, p. 251.

17. On this basic concept of the Kabbala see Gershom Scholem, "Kabbala," *Encyclopedia Judaica*, pp. 673 ff.; Ernst Müller, *Der Sohar und seine Lehre* (1923), p. 16; and others.

18. Nelson Glueck ("Das Wort *ḥesed* im alttestamentlichen Sprachgebrauche als menschliche und göttliche gemeinschaftsgemässe Ver-

side, and justice or judgment (*dīn*) on the left (feminine) side.[19] Mercy is associated with *water,* and justice with *fire.* The streaming waters of mercy overcome the consuming fire of judgment. The jealous God has literally gone to the "left" side. Here a deep view opens up into the essence of the process of divine development. It is only in his love that the masculine, creative side of God is manifested. His unpredictable emotionality, his wrath, his justice, are feminine. This is, psychologically speaking, the feminine side of God, which is undifferentiated and chaotic. The spiritual God Yahweh had struggled out of the maternal matrix of nature, the primal ground of pagan nature religions. Thereby the feminine side was necessarily suppressed but was manifested in his character unconsciously and negatively. Here the connection between the feminine and Satan becomes visible again. The "anger of Yahweh," in II Samuel 24 changes to "Satan" in I

---

haltungsweise," *BZAW* No. 47, 1927) points out the original legal character of *ḥesed.* In contrast to *raḥamīm,* to which it comes very close in the later (prophetic) period, *ḥesed* "includes the idea of dutifulness, which does not enter into *raḥamīm*" (p. 27; cf. also p. 66). W. F. Lofthouse ("*Hen* and *Hesed* in the Old Testament," *ZAW* [1933], pp. 29–35) by and large confirms Glueck's conclusions. But it seems doubtful to me whether Glueck, as regards the later development, has not stuck too close to the original meaning. The question is whether or not, at least for the *ḥesed* of God, a distinct further development in the sense of divine mercy and love took place. For instance, precisely in the passage quoted above, Ps. 86:15, where *ḥesed* appears as the synonym of *raḥūm we-ḥannūn, 'erek 'appaim:* "But thou, O Yahweh, art a God full of compassion, and gracious, long-suffering, and plenteous in mercy and truth." The purely formal connection seen by Lofthouse between *ḥesed* and *raḥamīm* can hardly suffice: "This word signifies yearning love; like that of a mother for the babe within her womb. . . . But even *raḥamīm* is based on a tie, indeed, the closest imaginable. Here *ḥesed* and *raḥamīm* are both in the nature of things" (*op. cit.,* p. 35). Cf. also the cited example of Jer. 3:12, in which Yahweh says of himself: "I am *ḥāsīd,*" where the direct continuation, "I will not keep anger forever," may certainly be seen as a direct explanation of the concept *ḥāsīd.* Surely this concept became in later Judaism the explicit expression for the flowing grace of God, as is shown by just the example in the Kabbala.

19. Cf. also the Chinese symbolism, where Yang is the light, Yin the dark, principle; light and darkness, day and night, as the balance of universal world forces in eternal movement.

Chronicles 21. In the same way, the "roaring lion," as the Old Testament image of the wrathful God (Hos. 11:10; Jer. 49:19), becomes the image of the *devil* in the New Testament (I Pet. 5:8).

However, what is fruitful in the Kabbala in this respect, and leading to further development, is that this feminine side, although on the "left," retains its whole dignity in the spiritual world system. The feminine is not only overcome, but is also accepted and retained in the sense of being preserved and essential. God embraces both his sides; he is masculine and feminine. He is the *coincidentia oppositorum.*

In Zechariah the conquering of justice by love is not yet complete. It is still in process. Justice as a potency is still embodied in Satan as the obstacle to God's mercy and goodness. But in that the *mal'āk Yahweh* opposes him, the way is opened for God's love to incline toward man. That God appears who wants to save "the brand plucked out of the fire," who has compassion for the people—sullied with sin and tormented with suffering, almost destroyed—represented by the high priest Joshua. For this live feeling, the dark emotionality becomes so suspect and negative that it appears as Satan, as a negative, destructive power. In view of this highly significant breakthrough of God's intervention for man, it is perhaps not sheer coincidence that the same chapter contains a reference to the Messiah (Zech. 3:8): "Hear now, O Joshua the high priest, thou and thy fellows that sit before thee; for they are men that are *a sign;* for, behold, I will bring forth My servant the *Shoot.*" [20]

In still another sense this passage represents a further development of the Satan concept in the Old Testament. We have seen that Satan is the element of hindrance which disturbs and

20. Italics added. For reasons of greater faithfulness to the Hebrew text this translation is taken from *The Holy Scriptures: A New Translation* (Philadelphia: The Jewish Publication Society of America, 1917). See also the Luther Bible: ". . . denn sie sind miteinander ein Wahrzeichen," and Zürich Bible: ". . . ihr seid Männer der Vorbedeutung."

obstructs the natural earthly life of men, that breaks their will (Balaam, Job) and leads them to submit to the will of God. But also this function now appears as limited. The religious feeling has penetrated deeper; there is a situation where even suffering is of no avail without God's mercy, where mercy must complete the work of suffering if God's vessel, man, is not to break. Satan, in his function of hindering, of breaking the human will and transforming it to submission to the will of God, has reached a limit where God must intervene to preserve the vessel. The *mal'āk Yahweh* rescues the "brand plucked out of the fire," the consuming fire of Yahweh. The loving God is able to protect man from the God of wrath. Job's prayer, "Lay down now; put me in a surety with thee," is here fulfilled, and with it his prophetic certainty: "I know that my Redeemer liveth." Joshua, the representative of the whole sinful people, is no more delivered up to Satan, as Job was. Does not this mean that man, once he has seen and borne the dark side of God, is no longer delivered up to it to the same degree?

Satan as Independent Demon (I Chronicles 21:1)

In I Chron. 21:1 it says: "And Satan stood up against Israel, and provoked David to number Israel." Satan appears here as instigator of an impious action, whose nature we must first establish.

That numbering the people was considered taboo is already shown in Exod. 30:11–16. There the census is not forbidden, but it is tolerated by Yahweh only if atonement is made for it at the same time:

> When thou takest the sum of the children of Israel after their number, then shall they give every man a ransom for his soul unto Yahweh, when thou numberest them; that there be no plague among them, when thou numberest them.

In itself, therefore, it is against the divine will—even, as it were, a mortal sin; for the lives forfeited by the counting have to be redeemed by a ransom; otherwise they fall victim to a plague which, as shown in I Chron. 21:11–12, is fatal.[1] David can choose the punishment for the numbering: famine, destruction by enemies, or pestilence. The census of the people must therefore imply a serious infringement of the divine power which calls forth the wrath of God. The census is by nature directed against the power of God because it serves human interests, the power of an earthly king. It makes him conscious of his power by putting it into his hands as a concrete, estimated value, and therewith only into his full

1. Cf. II Sam. 24:3, 4.

possession, as it were. Insofar as the census puts an emphasis on human possessions and human arrangements and planning, the census is a kind of disobedience to the ruling power of God, which is atoned for by an actual (II Sam. 24:3 and I Chron. 21:1) or symbolic (Exod. 30:11–16) sacrifice of life. This judgment of the census is very old and is found not only in the Bible. In the last analysis it is based on a widespread primitive idea, as J. G. Frazer has shown by many examples from Africa, America, and Europe.[2] Thus, the people in the Congo are afraid of being counted because it would attract the attention of evil spirits. Frazer mentions that a census taken there in 1908 for purposes of taxation had to be carried out by military force: "The natives would have resisted the officer, but he had too many soldiers with him; and it is not improbable that fights have taken place in other parts of Africa, not that they resisted the taxation, but they objected to be counted for fear the spirits would hear and kill them."[3] For the most part the dread extends to the counting of children, cattle, and other possessions. So, for instance, among the Bakongo in the lower Congo territory it is considered extremely unlucky for a woman to count her children—one, two, three, and so forth—for the evils spirits will hear it and take away some of them by death.[4] In East Africa the Masai count neither people nor cattle, in the belief that this causes death.[5] And in Oran (North Africa)

> the person who counts the measures of grain should be in a state of ceremonial purity, and instead of counting one, two, three, and so on, he says "in the name of God" for "one"; "two blessings" for "two"; "hospitality of the Prophet" for "three" . . . and so on, up to "twelve," for which the expression is "the perfection of God."[6]

2. J. G. Frazer, "The Sin of a Census," *Folklore in the Old Testament: Studies in Comparative Religion, Legend and Law* (1919), II, Ch. 9, 555 ff.

3. *Ibid.*, p. 556.

4. *Ibid.*

5. *Ibid.*

6. *Ibid.*, p. 558.

Bertheau[7] and Curtis[8] point to the *lustratio populi Romani*, established by Servius Tullius, which always took place on the Field of Mars after the completion of the census.[9] In his book *Die Beduinen von Beerseba*,[10] Leo Häfeli reports on the dread of a census among present-day Bedouins. The Governor of Beersheba, 'Āref el-'Āref, asserted that there were around 70,000 souls under the jurisdiction district of Bir es-Seba'. "Some believe there are more than 100,000. God knows what is correct!" Häfeli comments: "*Allah a'lam biṣ-ṣawab* or *'ilm 'ind Allah* are well known and often repeated formulations that bring to an end the discussion of a subject about which it is believed to be a wrong toward God to wish to investigate the exact facts." Karl Budde formulates this primitive idea very well as it relates to the sphere of the Old Testament: "The census is a direct attack on Israel, on the life of David's subjects. For Jahwe gives and takes away life; therefore he will not tolerate that one counts up his souls and, should one do so, he erases the computation by sending a great death."[11]

In our text this dread of the census is expressed by Joab (I Chron. 21:3): "Yahweh make his people an hundred times so many more as they be: but, my lord the king, are they not all my lord's servants? why then doth my lord require this thing? why will he be a cause of trespass to Israel?"[12]

Does this not voice the same attitude as that of the Bedouins of Beersheba? But David closes his ears to the genuinely God-fearing reproach of Joab. He follows the "sa-

7. *Die Bücher der Chronik* (Leipzig, 1873).

8. Curtis, *The Books of Chronicles* ("International Critical Commentary" series) (1910), p. 247.

9. Varro *De re rustica* II; Livy I. 44, cf. III. 22; Dionysius IV. 22; *cit.* Curtis, *loc. cit.*

10. (Lucerne, 1938), p. 25. I owe this reference to Prof. Zimmerli (lectures on Old Testament Theology, Zurich University, 1944–45).

11. K. Budde, *Die Bücher Samuel* (1902), p. 205, n. 21.

12. Since in our investigation the focus is on the figure of Satan, I will base the following exegesis only on the Chronicles text in which Satan is mentioned, although the Samuel text is older.

tanic" suggestion. However, his obsession, after the deed is done, is followed by a sense of guilt and remorse, all the deeper because of the cruel fact that the people have to pay for his—David's—guilt (I Chron. 21:17):

> Is it not I that commanded the people to be numbered? even I it is that have sinned and done evil indeed; but as for these sheep, what have they done? let thine hand, I pray thee, O Yahweh my God, be on me and on my father's house; but not on thy people . . .

It is this transformed David who then receives the command transmitted by Gad, the seer, to build Yahweh an altar—out of which later arose the Temple—which stood on the place where Yahweh commanded the angel who spread the plague to sheathe his sword, because "he repented him of the evil" (21:15). As with the Flood, the sacrifice of Isaac, and the trial of Job, we see Yahweh here, too, almost on the point of destroying his own creation. Again it is a matter of testing the carrier of salvation, as in Genesis 22, and of an inner transformation like Job's, although this story is much more primitive and is far from reaching the individual differentiation and depth of the Book of Job. However, the parallel is further expressed in the sparing of the future *place* of salvation; Jerusalem is at the last moment saved from destruction. If one thinks of the later central significance of Jerusalem, its high symbolic value in Ezekiel and later in Christianity, the importance of this passage can be fully recognized.[13] This Chronicles passage is also still more specifically connected with the Book of Job by the fact that in both Satan is the factor which sets destruction going. But what is new in

13. Cf. Karl Budde (*op. cit.*, p. 326) on the corresponding passage II Sam. 24:16: "Since now the sanctuary on Zion finally remained the only sanctuary of Yahweh, and became the only legitimate one according to the conviction of Israel, and then in its glorification and spiritualization passed into the possession of Christianity and in the New Testament Apocalypse was raised into the celestial world, one must designate this passage as one of the most important in the Old Testament." Cf. also Gerhard von Rad, art. "διάβολσο" in Kittel, *Theologisches Wörterbuch zum Neuen Testament,* II, 73, n. 17.

the Chronicles is that Satan is divested of his character as a *divine* function. He no longer appears, as in the Book of Job, as part of the divine court; he is an independent figure, apparently separated from God, who no longer stands in dialectic confrontation with God or his angel, as in Job and Zechariah. This is expressed linguistically by the fact that *śāṭān* has here become a proper name. In the divine process of differentiation, the detachment and becoming-visible of the dark side of God have now reached a state of complete separation. It appears now as a completely "autonomous complex," a separate *personality*.[14]

This fact has in various quarters given rise to the idea of a Persian influence. Gerhard von Rad [15] sees in it an "inner shift

14. In view of these highly meaningful connections, it is difficult to bring any understanding to the attempt of F. X. Kugler (*Von Mose bis Paulus, Forschungen zur Geschichte Israels* [1922], pp. 241–43) to see in the Satan of the Chronicles a *human* adversary of David's. But his argumentation has so little to sustain it that it can scarcely be taken seriously. To begin with, starting from a conception of God imposed upon the text, it is simply decided that the tempting of David could not have proceeded from God: "But can it be said of *Yahweh jāset* that 'he provoked [David]'? Certainly not in the sense that he is to be held the instigator of sin. . . . Therefore it seems to me very improbable that Yahweh is thought of here as the subject" (p. 242). Kugler grasps for a way out by assuming another subject, namely, the indefinite "one." Thus: "One provoked David." This, despite his admission that " 'one' is mostly expressed by the third person masculine plural and less frequently by the third person masculine singular" (*loc. cit.*). "Accordingly David would have been under the influence of a *bad adviser*. . . . He has probably accused the people to David of largely avoiding its obligations, and as a reliable countermeasure put through a general military [!] levy. So he became a Satan in the literal sense of the word, an accuser and persecutor of Israel" (pp. 242–43). Kaupel (*Die Dämonen des Alten Testaments* [1930]) has taken over this view of Kugler's and is not surpassed by him in the fantastic description of this human "Satan." I Chronicles 21 is supposed to refer to an "irresponsible intriguer" (p. 10), a "dark wire-puller" (p. 108). "This secret malicious agitator, against whose insinuations and machinations even Joab's urgent words to the king were of no avail, is called *śāṭān* in I Chron. 21:1." After this "solution" of the problem, Kaupel states with obvious relief: "So the passage, which for many expositors has signified the high point or at least an important step forward in the Old Testament Satan concept, is eliminated from consideration of this subject."

15. *Op. cit.*, p. 74.

in the Satan concept which perhaps came about as the result of newly penetrated Iranian ideas," but he emphasizes that "the Satan concept was by no means 'taken over' from the Persians."[16] In contrast to this view, Erik Stave[17] sees in Angra Mainyu the primal image of the Old Testament Satan, thereby going further than his predecessor, Alexander Kohut,[18] who on the whole restricts the Parsistic influence to the Satan of the Apocrypha and the Talmud. Stave, too, sees the immanent factor along with the assumed Persian influence; but with him the two points of view do not yet fuse into a unified picture but remain occasionally—and this just in regard to the problem of the origin of the Satan figure—in open contradiction to each other.

In addition to all the results of our investigations which speak against a "taking-over" of the Satan figure, as far as the "Persian" thesis is concerned, a comparison of the basic structures of the two religions suffices for us to consider, with von Rad and others, that such a "taking-over" is out of the question.

If one looks at the two figures—that of the Old Testament Satan and of the Angra Mainyu of the Persian religion—not as separate entities but as embedded in the whole religious pattern, a fundamental difference is apparent. Stave, too, starts from the premise that the Old Testament Satan from the outset did not have the same character as the Persian Angra Mainyu. The latter is from the beginning an independent power beside Ahura Mazda. In the Persian religion there exists a primary opposition between Spenta Mainyu and Angra Mainyu. Angra Mainyu, like Ahura Mazda, reigns over his own realm, and the two wage war on each other. They also share in the creation of the physical universe, since Angra

16. Cf. also Scheftelowitz, *Die altpersische Religion und das Judentum* (Giessen, 1920), p. 51: "The assumption that the Jews have taken this idea from the Persians is untenable."

17. *Ueber den Einfluss des Parsismus auf das Judentum* (Haarlem, 1898).

18. *Ueber die jüdische Angelologie und Dämonologie in ihrer Abhängigkeit vom Parsismus* (1866).

Mainyu participates in the creation. He is the creator of harmful insects and animals.[19] In Yasna 45, 2 it says: "Yea, I will declare the world's two first spirits . . ."; [20] in Farvardin-Yast XXII, 76: ". . . when the two spirits created the world, the Good Spirit and the Evil One." [21] And in Yasna 30, 3 they are called a pair: [22] "Thus are the primeval spirits who as a pair . . . have been famed [of old]." [23]

Hence, for the Persian religion, dualism is the *point of departure.* The cosmic-ethical conflict appears to have been the fundamental experience of the Persians, giving their religion its shape. In contrast, it seems to me (as I have pointed out earlier; see above, p. 10) that the specific creative factor in the religion of the Israelite people was something quite opposite: the personality-quality of God, as the unity which embraces and resolves the opposites.

Departing from this basic consideration, any unprejudiced observer will soon realize that an influence of Ahriman-Angra Mainyu upon the figure of Satan is eminently present. It is not, however, at the Old Testament level, where Satan is, as it were, born out of the Old Testament figure of God, but at a further stage of development: the late Judeo-Christian. Only in Satan as the adversary of the Messiah in late Jewish writings, on the one hand, and in the New Testament, on the other, can Angra Mainyu be recognized as the proto-

19. Vendidad, ch. 1. See *Sacred Books of the East,* ed. F. Max Müller, 2d ed., IV: *The Zend-Avesta* (Oxford, 1895), p. 198, trans. James Darmesteter.

20. *Sacred Books of the East,* ed. F. Max Müller, (Oxford, 1887), XXXI, 125, trans. L. H. Mills.

21. *Sacred Books of the East,* ed. F. Max Müller, (Oxford, 1883), XXIII, 198, trans. James Darmesteter.

22. Rendered "a pair of twins" by Fritz Wolff in his German translation, *Avesta: Die heiligen Bücher der Parsen, übersetzt auf der Grundlage von Chr. Bartholomae's altiranischem Wörterbuch* (1924), p. 240: "Die beiden Geister zu Anfang, die sich durch ein Traumgesicht als Zwillingspaar offenbarten. . . ."

23. *Sacred Books of the East,* ed. F. Max Müller, (1887), XXXI, 29, trans. L. H. Mills.

type of Satan. Here Satan has become an independent principle, the embodiment of evil as a world principle. Therefore Gunkel has some justification for discriminating the Old Testament Satan completely from Satan in the New Testament.[24] He believes that the two figures are independent of each other and derive from different origins, the New Testament Satan stemming from Persian influence. Carried to this extreme conclusion, his opinion becomes inaccurate, however. It is indispensable to take both factors into account, that of continuity *and* that of difference, and this is possible only by means of the concept of development. It would be absurd to assume, for a time and place shaped by Yahwism, the inception of a spiritual concept which had no relation to it; the more so since the continuity of the name also presents an indication, even though only an external one, for the inner continuity of the Satan figure in the Old and New Testaments.

It becomes clear, therefore, that only a differentiation in the divine personality, almost tantamount to falling apart, could form the prerequisite for a more penetrating Persian influence, i.e., the *end* phase of the process of enfolding of the Old Testament godhead, but not its beginning. To this extent a Persian influence, such as von Rad also takes into consideration, might perhaps be possible as early as the passage in Chronicles.[25] Ahriman, in his polar opposition to Ahura Mazda, may have been a prototype for the Old Testament Satan detaching himself from the personality of God. Here too, however, the decisive factor is the immanent development as a prerequisite for such an influence. Only after this differentiation process had taken place was the ground pre-

24. Gunkel, "Teufelsglaube," *RGG* ², V, 1063–64.

25. Cf. also G. Kittel (*Geschichte des Volkes Israel* [1927], III, 141), who assumes a Persian influence already for the Satan of Zechariah, although he does not hold "an independent inner Jewish further development of the earlier concept" to be precluded. In my opinion these two possibilities are not mutually exclusive.

pared for a further-reaching Persian influence, which can be clearly traced in the texts.[26]

The detachment of Satan from God, who is then "cleansed" of his darkness, carried tremendous consequences. It formed the premise for the New Testament development of Satan into the contrapersonality of God and for his complete splitting-off, as this is expressed in the mythologem of the "bound" dragon of the Apocalypse.

In the Old Testament as his "birthplace," Satan's connection with God is still discernible even in the Chronicles pas-

26. So in Wisd. of Sol. 2:24 Satan appears identical with the Paradise serpent and death. Later Judaism also knows this conception. In the Talmud, Satan is also the "Angel of Death" (Baba Bathra 16a; Jer. Sabb. 2, 6; etc.; see Scheftelowitz, *op. cit.*, p. 56, n. 7). And by the rabbis the devil is also called *han-naḥaš haq-qādmōn* (Weber, *System der altsynagogalen palästinensischen Theologie*, pp. 211 f., *cit.* Stave, *op. cit.*, p. 266. Cf. also Kohut, *op. cit.*, p. 66. The extremely interesting contrast to Adam Kadmon cannot be dealt with here.) These traits correspond very exactly to the Persian Ahriman. With him death enters the world: "[Yea] when the two spirits came together at the first to make life, and life's absence. . . ." (Yasna 30, 4. See *Sacred Books of the East*, ed. F. Max Müller [Oxford, 1887], XXXI, 30, trans. L. H. Mills); and in the Vendidad, ch. 1, he has the standing epithet "who is all death" (*Sacred Books of the East*, ed. F. Max Müller [Oxford, 1895], IV, 4 ff.). About his serpent form, the Bundehesh, chapter 3, says: "Afterwards, the evil spirit, with the confederate demons, went towards the luminaries and he saw the sky; and he led them up, fraught with malicious intentions. He stood upon one-third of the inside of the sky, and he sprang like a snake out of the sky down to the earth" (*Pahlavi Texts in the Sacred Books of the East*, ed. F. Max Müller, [1880], V, 17, trans. E. W. West). See further correspondences between Ahriman and the late Jewish-Christian Satan in Scheftelowitz, *op. cit.*, pp. 55 ff.; Stave, *op. cit.*, pp. 263 ff.; Kohut, *op. cit.*, pp. 62 ff.; Roskoff, *Geschichte des Teufels* (1869), pp. 190 ff.

Instructive in our context is the fact that there is evidence of the direct adoption of a Persian demon in the post-Exilic period—not of Satan, however, but of *Asmodi* in the Book of Tobit, which probably originated in Persia. It is typical that here, as with the ancient Babylonian demons, the name is also retained; according to the most general view, Asmodi is the Persian Aeshma Daeva. According to Alexander Kohut (*op. cit.*, p. 73), Aeshma is called "the violently seeking, desirous spirit." So the example of Asmodi in regard to the Persian stage of assimilation, as well as that of the cacodemons of the Old Testament in regard to the Babylonian, supports our conception of the Old Testament Satan as a phenomenon within the divine sphere.

sage. If our previous investigations of the Chronicles account have already, by the parallels which offered themselves, brought Satan in essence very close to Yahweh, this relationship is revealed again with unexpected profundity in II Sam. 24:1 ff. In his independence in I Chronicles 21, Satan is no longer related to God, because he is, as it were, identical with him. He does exactly what Yahweh himself does in II Sam. 24:1. There it says: "And again the *anger of Yahweh* was kindled against Israel, and he moved David against them . . ." [27] (italics added). Thus in the Book of Samuel it is clearly Yahweh who himself provokes the man David to sin against him. From this background of the ambivalence of the divine personality itself—which may be considered another express confirmation of the thesis of this book, that Satan embodies a side of God's being—the corresponding inner divine tension between Yahweh and Satan in the Chronicles becomes fully apparent. The census is against the will of Yahweh, it is hubris, disobedience of man, but, as *Satan*, Yahweh himself

27. It is probably not necessary in our context to go into the problem of the literary connection between I Chronicles 21 and II Samuel 24. Even if II Samuel 24 is not the source of the Chronicler, as assumed by Rothstein (*Kommentar zum ersten Buch der Chronik* [1927], pp. 285 ff.), J. Benzinger (*Die Bücher der Chronik* [1901], p. 62), and, to a limited extent, also K. Budde (*op. cit.*, p. 327)—M. Noth has an opposing view (*Ueberlieferungsgeschichtliche Studien*, I [1943], 138); he even thinks that the Chronicler had nothing before him but the Book of Samuel in the form which tradition handed down—this would in no way affect the *inner* relation between the two passages, which alone concerns us here. They present two stages of a theological development. This is fully acknowledged by Rothstein, too, despite his aforementioned judgment in regard to the literary problem, when he says: "Here Satan corresponds to the wrath in Yahweh's innermost being which is enflamed against Israel and seductively incites David to count the people. Thus, the divine wrath was, as it were, incarnated in him, separated from Yahweh, and had become an independent personality. This detachment of the wrathful reaction to sin in God's divine being from the divine personality as such, and its hypostatization in the figure of Satan, naturally was not accomplished overnight; it needed a process of development extending over a considerable time before it became possible to reshape the old account in its beginning in the form now offered us by the writer of Chronicles" (Rothstein, *op. cit.*, pp. 379–80.)

leads man into this sin. If we think of the role established for Satan so far, we may also justifiably surmise a divine purpose in the temptation of David into sin. If in Genesis 3 we have found this ambivalence of God, who does not want man to eat of the tree of knowledge lest he become like God and yet through the serpent tempts him to do so—here still, so to speak, "unconsciously"—because man's godlike knowledge of good and evil is just what God really desires (see above, pp. 130 f.); and if, in the stories of Balaam and Job, we have seen Satan as the force that, by breaking man's will, makes him conscious of his own will in the clash with God's, then we may here suspect the same goal—namely, man's becoming conscious—as the "meaning of the sin." David's royal power is obviously decimated as a result of the guilt effected by Satan. Only consciousness of it creates room in David for the will of God and makes David the carrier of revelation. Satan here really proves himself to be a "demonic-destructive principle firmly anchored in the plan of salvation," as von Rad formulates it so well in reference to I Chronicles 21.[28] Even the Chronicler, who usually has no great compunction about whitewashing the sins of "good" kings (for instance, he never mentions the Bath-sheba story [29]) cannot avoid including David's sin and his emphatic confession of guilt. David's confession of guilt goes hand in hand with Yahweh's command to the angel of pestilence to desist. The enantiodromia in the human soul corresponds to that in the divine personality. It is as if here were the first small seed of the much later identification of the human soul with the "heavenly Jerusalem." For in medieval Christianity the heavenly Jerusalem became the symbol of the redeemed soul, and the walled city the symbol of the soul which had come into its own and therewith, at the same time, to God. David builds the altar from which the temple shall rise. In the later stage of Job it is already the soul that finds itself in God. Through David, Jerusalem becomes "the house of Yahweh the

28. Von Rad, *op. cit.*, p. 74.
29. Cf. II Samuel 11 and I Chronicles 20.

God" (I Chron. 22:1); with Job it is the human soul. But this is what we have already recognized to be the final, urgent goal of the activity manifested in Satan: the human soul as "dwelling-place" of the God becoming conscious of himself.

INDEX